Frontier Metropolises

Tulsa, Indian Territory & Tel Aviv, Palestine

By

BENJAMIN A. LAWSON

Indian University Press

Published by
Indian University Press at
Bacone College
Muskogee, Oklahoma
http://www.bacone.edu/indian-university-press

4521_3

Designed by Benjamin A. Lawson
Cover design by Benjamin A. Lawson and Aihua Zheng

ISBN 978-0-9772448-3-6

Printed in the United States of America

Contents

For

Mum and Dad

and

Aihua

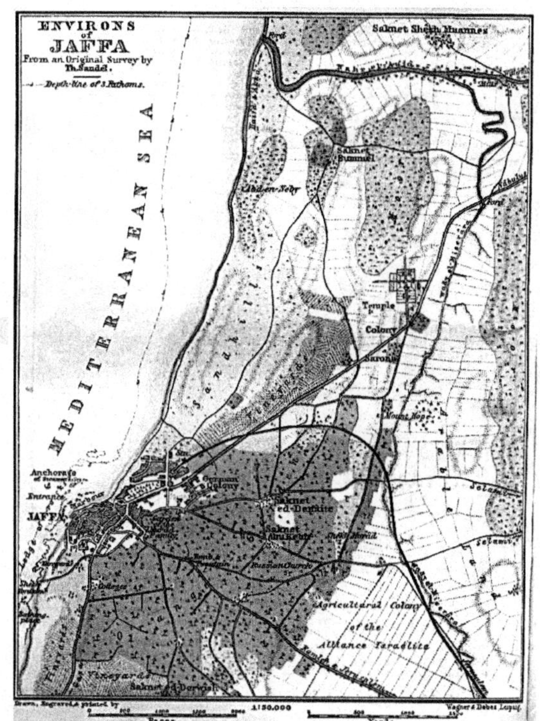

Jaffa Environs (including Tel Aviv), 1912

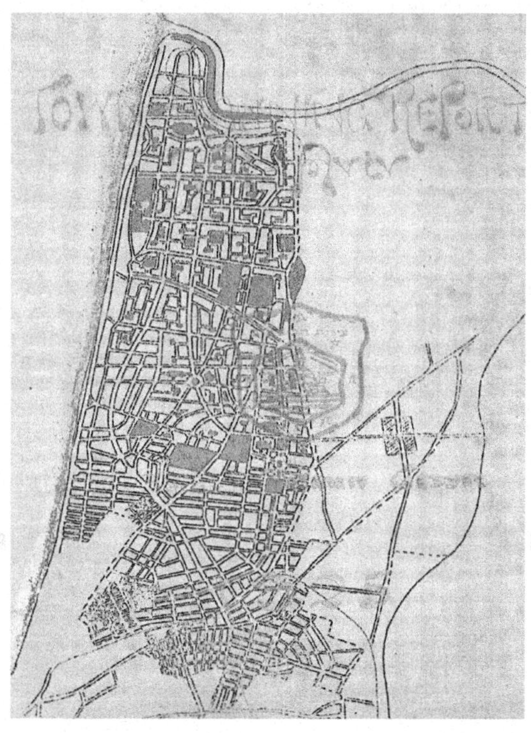

Tel Aviv Plan, 1925

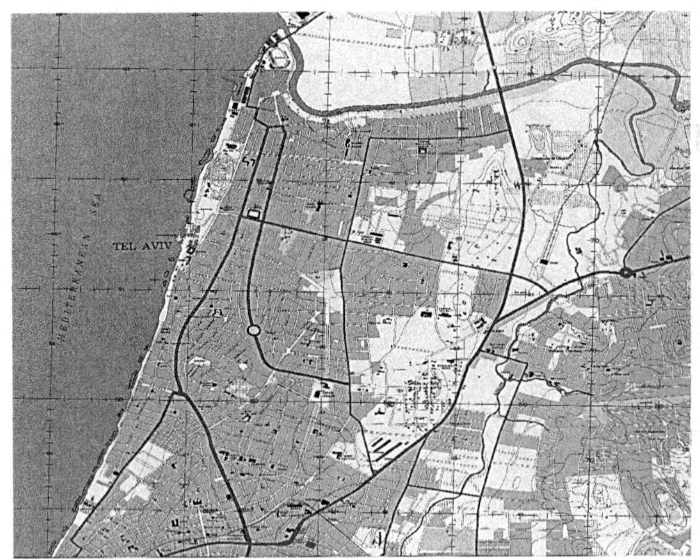

Tel Aviv Map, north, 1950s

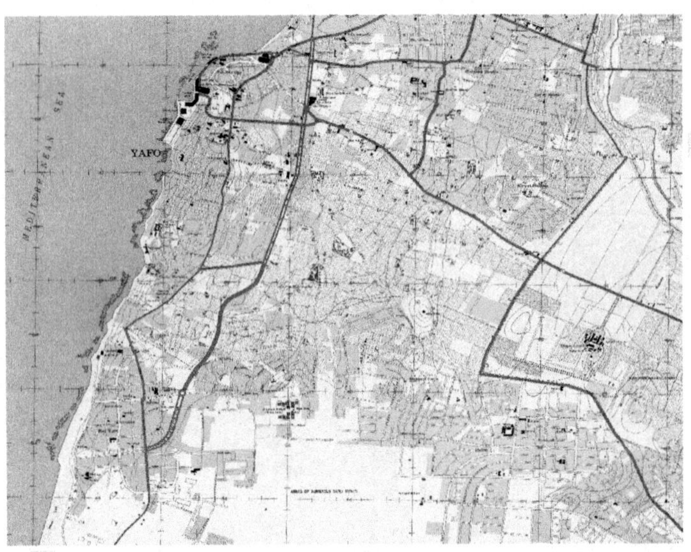

Tel Aviv Map, south, 1950s

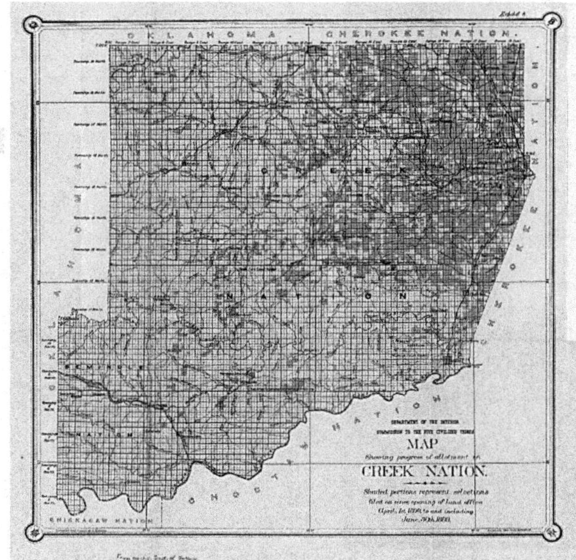

Creek Lands (Tulsa is in the top center), 1890s

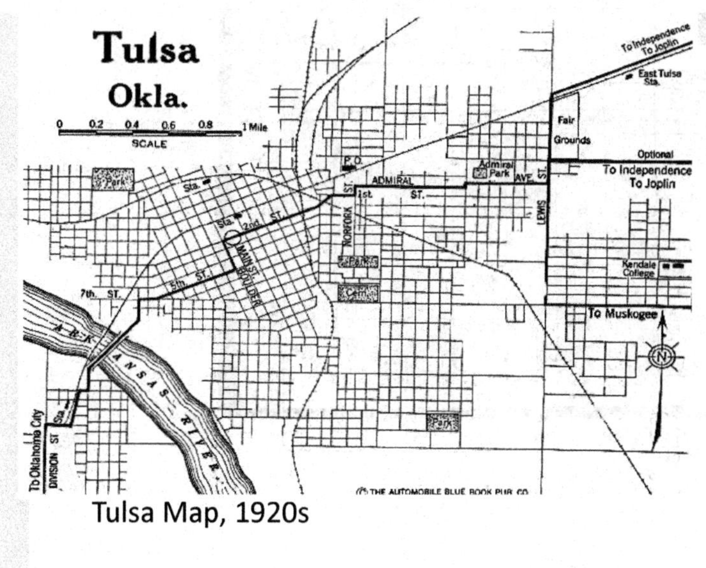

Tulsa Map, 1920s

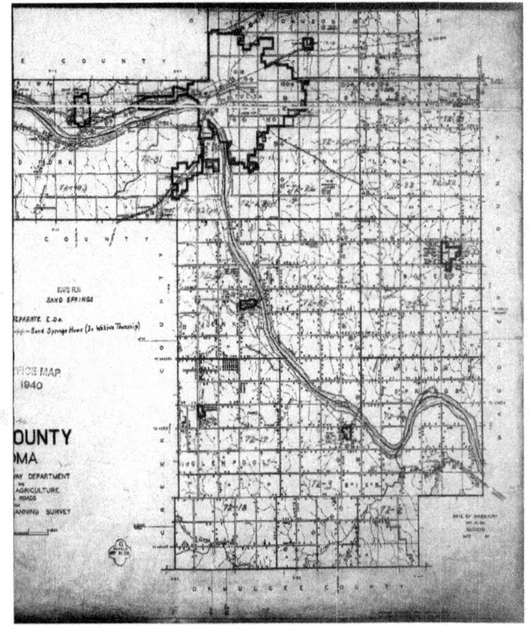

Tulsa County Map, 1940s

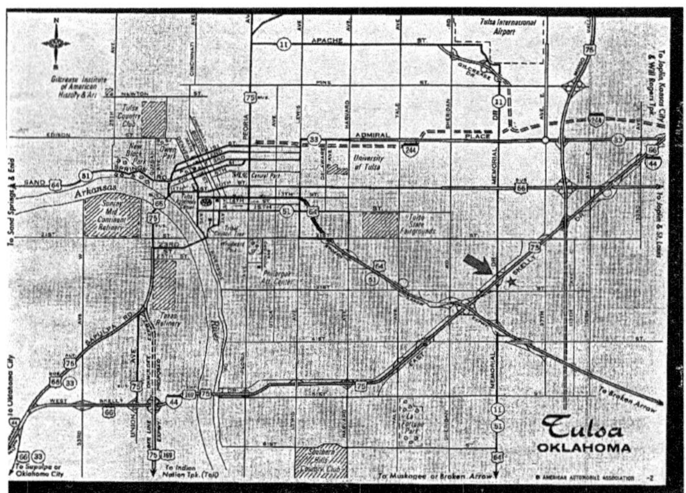

Tulsa Map, 1960s

Chapter One

Myths

Tel Aviv and Tulsa

The story begins as competition over land, and becomes one of aggressive civic promotion and a careful re-interpreting of the past. Tel Aviv (תל אביב), established 1909, and Tulsa, incorporated 1898, were the centers of Western-style settlement in the areas of Palestine and Indian Territory, before these areas became today's Israel and Oklahoma. In the decades after their founding, Tel Aviv and Tulsa flourished economically, due to advantages of the landscape, immigration, and of industry. These two cities, however, relied on a myth: that they were "frontier" cities, and that their growth and success meant the triumph of "civilization." A frontier is a place where cultures meet; sometimes, through the form of violence, other times through inter-mixing and exchange. A frontier is also a symbol, and a myth; one of the strengths of a myth—i.e. a foundational story that explains the status quo--is that it does not require truth to be powerful or effective.

Presenting Tel Aviv and Tulsa as "frontier" cities—i.e. the edge of Western Civilization--was a central part of the founding myth that enabled them to develop so quickly as self-styled modern, Westernized cities. In Palestine and Indian Territory, the growth of Tel Aviv and Tulsa meant encroachment on the land, livelihood, and rights of the indigenous peoples. The founding myths sought to hide the historical fact of existing non-Western settlement and to downplay competing claims to the land--to say the land in question was "desert" and ripe for urban settlement.

The ideologies of Zionism (ציונית) and Manifest Destiny played a huge role in justifying the takeover of land in Palestine and the interior of North America. These ideologies allowed the newcomers to argue that their right to the land superseded the right of peoples already occupying the land. These ideologies cast settlement as the "greater good," an unavoidable progress, a process smiled upon by God. The Jews justified this claim by pointing to the *Torah* (תורה), in which their ancestors—including Abraham, Jacob, Moses, David and Solomon—lived, fought over, and ruled the lands of Palestine. In this holy tradition, on several occasions God explicitly grants the Jewish people the right to that land. In *Genesis*, for example, God tells Abraham:

> your name shall be Abraham; for I have made you the ancestor of a multitude of nations. I will make you exceedingly fruitful; and I will make nations of you, and kings shall come from you. I will establish my covenant between me and you, and your offspring after you throughout their generations, for an everlasting covenant, to be God to you and to your offspring after you. And I will give to you, and to your offspring after you, the land where you are now an alien, all the land of Canaan, for a perpetual holding; and I will be their God.[1]

In the following books of the *Torah*, God repeatedly renewed this covenant with Abraham's (Jewish) descendants--the most significant was with Moses after he brought the Hebrews out of Egypt.

Zionism was a secular and political ideology, connected with Judaism through ethnic identity (i.e. as Jews) rather than through religion (i.e. as believers in Judaism), but it drew from the stories of the *Torah* to justify Jewish colonization of Palestine.

The Zionist movement began as a reaction to increasing Anti-Semitism in Europe, which had been an on-and-off problem in Europe for centuries but became more systematic and widespread in the nineteenth century; examples like the Dreyfus Affair and the forged anti-Semitic document *The Protocols of the Elders of Zion* made the political situation in Europe seem hostile to Jews. Nationalism, in the wake of the French revolution, and the unification of Italy and Germany, made one's nation a primary means of identity and purpose—and often defined nations as areas defined by a common language or heritage; Jews were often excluded by this sort of rhetoric. Many well-educated Jews began advocating for the creation of a "National Home" or "Jewish State" as the best long-term

---

[1] Genesis, 7:3-8.

solution, and the Zionist movement was born. The World Zionist Organization (ההסתדרות הציונית העולמית) was founded in 1897. One of the early Zionist leaders was Theodore Herzl, a journalist living in Vienna, who advocated the Jews' return to their ancestral/ancient homeland: Palestine. Another important figure was Eliezer Ben-Yehuda, who worked tirelessly to resurrect the ancient language of Hebrew; Hebrew was still the traditional, holy, language but was no longer spoken.

For the European-born Jews who began the Zionist movement at the close of the nineteenth century, the physical land of Palestine had ingrained nationalist significance. Zionists acted on the belief that it was imperative for European Jews to found a Jewish State in Palestine, their historical geographical homeland. As Herzl explained, only Palestine—and not an alternative such as Argentina--would do: "With money [provided to facilitate Jewish settlement outside of Palestine] you cannot make a general movement of a great mass of people. You must give them an ideal. You must put into them the belief in their future, and then you will be able to take out of them the devotion to the hardest labour imaginable…In Palestine they [the Jews following the Zionist call] work with enthusiasm and they succeed."[2]

Similarly, Americans often viewed their settlement of North America as a parallel to the Biblical stories of the ancient Jews. At the founding of the Massachusetts Bay Colony in 1630, John Winthrop declared the soon-to-be-established settlement of Boston as a "City upon a hill" chosen by God to be a light, or example for the world. Citing the *New Testament* (Matthew 5:14, "Ye are the light of the world. A city that is set on a hill cannot be hid"), in his sermon "A Model of Christian Charity" Winthrop said:

> We shall find that the God of Israel is among us, when ten of us shall be able to resist a thousand of our enemies; when He shall make us a praise and glory that men shall say of succeeding plantations, "may the Lord make it like that of New England. For we must consider that we shall be as a city upon a hill. The eyes of all people are upon us. So that if we shall deal falsely with our God in this work we have undertaken, and so cause

[2] Martin Gilbert, *Israel: A History* (New York: Harper Perennial, 2008), 21.

> Him to withdraw His present help from us, we shall be made a story and a by-word through the world."[3]

This sort of attitude gradually translated into the 1800s concept of "Manifest Destiny," which was a general term for America's land-hungry movement westward across the continent; journalist John O'Sullivan coined the phrase "Manifest Destiny" in 1839 and the name stuck. This ideology justified America's reneging on treaties with Native Americans and Mexico, because the idea was that Americans had a natural right to settle the interior lands of North America—including today's Oklahoma.

The larger point about the ideologies of Zionism and Manifest Destiny is that they allowed the settlers to ignore all claims to the land but their own, without guilt. For both Tulsa and Tel Aviv, the myths of Zionism and Manifest Destiny were part of a concerted plan to promote a specific image, based on accepting a myth as fact.

Tulsa Booster Party, 1908

The means of promoting, and ultimately realizing the fruition of this mythical ideal were simple: the booster myths (i.e. civic promotion) justified the takeover of land, representations were the means of giving the myths life, and the actual building of cities made the myths seem real. In Tel Aviv, the booster narrative

The Founding of Tel Aviv: Ahuzat Bayit, 1909

[3] John Winthrop, A Model of Christian Charity, 1630.

was captured through means of photography and drawings that literally ignored the neighboring city of Jaffa (יפו or Yafo in Hebrew), in order to show the Zionist settlers of Tel Aviv--known at first as Ahuzat Bayit (אחוזת בית) or "homestead"—as settling a desert area, on the sand dunes near the Mediterranean Sea; for example, the famous artist Nachum Gutman drew pictures of Tel Aviv that ignored Jaffa. In Tulsa, the focus was on suggesting that Native Americans did not live on the actual site of the American settlement; artists painted pictures of the "heroic" myths of cowboys and of oilmen, or venture capitalists making a fortune in the wilderness. Most significantly, the early land use patterns of Tulsa and Tel Aviv were the means of normalizing the often-hostile takeover of land. The booster rhetoric and promotion of the settlement of Tel Aviv and Tulsa are clear examples of how American and Zionist settlers posited themselves as the civilized people who were venturing into the savage frontier to serve as a "light for the world." This ideological justification was focused on actually settling the land, and solidifying the claim to civilization by creating cities. Building Tel Aviv and Tulsa in a

Jaffa, 19th Century

highly regularized and segregated fashion was an attempt at literally making the modern myth (of the superiority of European-derived development patterns) a reality.

Tulsa and Tel Aviv grew out of a longer history of urban settlement patterns; there were clear examples for them to follow. As the historian Richard Wade pointed out in his seminal book on St. Louis, Pittsburg and other frontier cities that preceded Tulsa by over a century, imitating existing urban trends gave "the illusion of orderliness," which settlers associated with cities in the U.S. eastern seaboard or in Western Europe.[4]

Western (i.e. European-derived) urban-development strategies changed dramatically in the mid-nineteenth century, when European city planners developed specific styles of (re)building cities, as part of the "modernization" or "regularization" of city blocks and infrastructure. These techniques, circa 1890, included underground sewers, street-grid patterns, wide boulevards, and grand monuments and buildings. These styles originated in Europe's grand cities like Paris and London, but quickly spread elsewhere in Europe and throughout Europe's network of colonies, allies, and competitors. The Ottoman Empire, which controlled Palestine, and the United States of America, which sought to control as much of the North American continent as possible, both adopted these newly fashionable city-building techniques.

Implementing European-style development infrastructure--orderly street grids, sanitary sewers, fire-code compliant buildings, and beautiful vistas of grand monuments--were all means of proclaiming one's attainment of ideals like progress, civilization, and the positive influence of the existing government. Viewed thusly, it makes sense why architecture, urban planning, and European concepts of land settlement and development became tools of conquest in contested areas like Palestine and Indian Territory. Establishing new cities—of which Tel Aviv and Tulsa were the most successful and important—created the essential foothold that European-Zionist and American settlers needed. The urban settlements of Tel Aviv and Tulsa allowed the newcomers to create the narrative that their urban development patterns were both justified and flourishing.

[4] Richard Wade, *The Urban Frontier* (Chicago: The University of Chicago Press, 1959), 27.

Urban planning and land-development patterns had political ramifications. Therefore, analyzing the two major urban settlements in Palestine and Indian Territory showcases the (ongoing) tensions of the areas in a unique light. First of all, drawing out the similarities and differences of North America and Palestine helps to illustrate an essential insight: these two situations are part of a larger context of westernization, and of modernization under the European model. Secondly, focusing on Tel Aviv and Tulsa brings the issues of land, development, and settlement into sharp focus; different conceptions of land use and ownership, especially settlement and development techniques, were major sources of misunderstanding and tension.

Tel Aviv began as a collection of small Jewish neighborhoods, which were essentially suburbs of the ancient seaport city of Jaffa. Jaffa at the beginning of the twentieth century was majority Arab, but cosmopolitan, and was considered an important, if frontier, city of the Istanbul-based Ottoman Empire. Legally, Jews who were not Ottoman subjects were restricted from purchasing land under Ottoman rule, but transactions occurred in and near Jaffa regardless. Neve Tzedek, the first of the Jewish neighborhoods, was purchased in 1886 and was settled in 1887; soon after Tel Aviv was officially founded in 1909 it combined with the earlier Jewish neighborhoods.

The main street in early Tel Aviv was Herzl Street, on a north-south axis, which ended at the Herzliya Hebrew Gymnasium (High School), Tel Aviv's most significant early building, for which the cornerstone was laid in 1909. The architectural style of the early Jewish neighborhoods was in stark contrast to the modernist style of the 1930s. In 1910s and 1920s Tel Aviv, the architectural style was more Mediterranean, with red tile roofs.

Land speculation drove prices up in 1912, and this was one of the major factors that led to Tel Aviv's growth into a city. Increased (illegal) Jewish immigration to Tel Aviv was part of the Zionist movement's plan to create successful settlements in Palestine with the intention of establishing a Jewish State there. This Zionist program was race/ethnicity based, and was a direct offshoot of European Imperialism and the European Enlightenment.

Tel Aviv quickly became the foothold the Zionists needed to hold their settlements together in Palestine and promote a unified face to the outside world. Tel Aviv was named after the Hebrew translation of Theodore Herzl's book *Altneuland*; Tel Aviv symbolically means Old/New land because tel refers to the mound of an ancient city and aviv means spring. Tel Aviv was from the beginning an utopian settlement, promoted as a major city long before it took shape—international Zionist organizations such as Keren Hayesod (קרן היסוד), the Jewish National Fund, and the Jewish Colonial Trust were instrumental in this promotional scheme. The leaders of Zionism were well-connected in Europe, and had access to powerful persons; for example, Chaim Weizmann (who became Israel's first president) had the ear of Lord Balfour, head of British policy in Palestine. By the time that the British took control of Palestine, following the defeat of the Ottoman Empire in World War One, the Zionists had established a firm grip on the British political establishment--culminating in the Balfour Declaration of 1917 which established the Jewish State in Palestine under the British Mandate--and Tel Aviv was their primary city. Although in reality a small frontier city, dwarfed by the neighboring and already somewhat modernized city of Jaffa, Tel Aviv was poised to grow exponentially. During the 1910s-1920s the mass immigration of Jews was a contentious sore point between the Ottomans, the British, the

Herzl Street and the Gymnasium, 1920s

Zionists, and the Palestinian Arabs. Measures were legally in place to limit Jewish immigration to Palestine, but these measures were difficult to enforce at all times; the British failure to effectively enforce these laws angered and frustrated the local Arabs, who by this time (the 1920s and 1930s) saw the mass migration of European Jews to Palestine as a direct threat to their political influence and economic livelihood. Skirmishes broke out sporadically in these decades between Arab and Jew, which led to an escalating division between the groups.

By the mid-1930s, when Tel Aviv began its Bauhaus, or International Style development project—the basis of what is today known as the "White City"—the municipality of Tel Aviv had implemented measures, including a wall, to divide Tel Aviv from the predominately Arab neighborhoods of Jaffa. The widespread commissioning of Modernist Architecture was a different type of wall constructed between Tel Aviv and (Arab) Jaffa: a myth, based on architectural symbolism. The symbolism of the cutting-edge European-style modern buildings and of grand boulevards like Rothschild Boulevard proclaimed that Tel Aviv was a thoroughly progressive and civilized city on par with Europe's great cities.

Tulsa grew out of the migrations of many peoples to the Arkansas River valley. Historically, the area of Tulsa was a mixture of myriad peoples. Circa 1800, Native American tribes living in the area were the Wichitas, Caddos, Plains Apaches, and Quapas; new tribes relocating to the area prior to 1830 were the Osage, Comanche, Pawnee, and Kiowa. Circa 1800-1830, French traders and American explorers maintained a semi-permanent presence in the general region of Tulsa--especially in the area of Ft. Gibson (est. 1824), located at the Three Forks: the meeting of the Arkansas, Verdigris, and Grand rivers. River travel was the easiest and most practical means of transportation at this time, before the invention and expansion of railroads (in the late-19th century); the Arkansas River was not easily navigated north of the Three Forks and so the trip to Tulsa was difficult. The U.S. policy of seizing tribal land reached new heights in 1830 with the Indian Removal Act and the subsequent re-location of the Five Civilized Tribes (Creek, Seminole, Chickasaw, Choctaw, and Cherokee) to Indian Territory. In 1836 a displaced band of Creeks (the Lochapoka) settled down near the banks of the Arkansas River, at the future site of Tulsa, to recreate their original home town; the site they chose was near a large Oak Tree: known as the Council Oak. The Civil War (1860-1865) disrupted Native American settlements in Indian Territory, and the constant westward movement of American settlers threatened tribal lands. As more white Americans settled illegally in Indian Territory, many tribes felt betrayed, but could do little to stop the migration. The U.S. government, instead of honoring its treaties, passed legislation encouraging increased American settlement; for example, the Dawes Act (1887) made Native Americans legally American citizens but forced tribes to split up their block allocations of land into specific tracts among eligible members, and opened much of the remaining land to American settlers through land runs (through the 1889 Indian Appropriation Act) or purchase.

In 1882, with the construction of a railroad spur from Vinita to the Arkansas River, the American settlement of Tulsa began. One of the reasons for selecting the site of Tulsa was the fact that the area was in Creek territory, just over the boundary from Cherokee holdings; the Creeks had a more lenient land-holding policy for non-tribal affiliated settlers. Legally, whites were prohibited from possessing land in both Creek and Cherokee holdings except for settlers who married Native American women and attained tribal status. For men not taking that route, the Creek nation's more lenient land-holding policy meant a significant benefit: thus the settlement site of Tulsa in Creek territory. In the following decades, Tulsa, popularly called "Tulsey Town," flourished as a frontier trading outpost, especially as a stop on the cattle drives from Texas, which led to increased Anglo-American settlement; Tulsa was officially incorporated in 1898. The construction of the railroad spur in 1882 made Tulsa a regional transportation hub, and encouraged Anglo-American merchants to move into Tulsa and set up shop. Some of Tulsa's early founders and oil men were part-Indian, notably: the descendants of Chief Benjamin Perryman, including Josiah Perryman who was Tulsa's first postmaster; Jeff Archer, one of the original 1882 settlers who opened a general store. Nevertheless, the city of Tulsa developed nearly exclusively in an American, European-based fashion. For example, one of Tulsa's founders, J.M. Hall—who arrived in 1882--wrote a book about Tulsa's early days, *The Beginning of Tulsa* (1927, revised 1933), and took pains to emphasize that no settlement existed in the area before 1882; Hall cited testimony from local Indian men that only one Creek man, Reuben Partridge, had a house at the site of Tulsa, but besides that "no house could be seen here until about August 1, 1882."[5] Since J.M. Hall arrived in Tulsa in 1882, this account justified (for him) the *tabula rasa* of Tulsa's site; for Hall, Tulsa was totally an American town, where Native Americans had been in the general area but had not preempted American settlement of the specific site of Tulsa. Tulsa's growth spurt truly began in 1905 with the discovery of oil nearby at the Keifer-Glenn Pool—then the largest oil pool in the world. Tulsa was from the start an entrepreneurial city, a place where people came to do business and seek their fortune.

Tulsa took shape over the following decades, following the logic of frontier towns: simple structures, unpaved roads, and many businesses concentrated downtown to serve the often transient population. The style of buildings in early Tulsa was unprepossessing on the outside, but brazenly displaying wealth inside: the cattle trade (and later, after 1905, the oil business) meant that many patrons of Tulsa businesses had money to spend.

Tulsa, 1910

Surveyors of Tulsa's roads planned the grid layout of streets on a logical, geometric basis well before these "streets" were anything more than an imaginary line. The initial "downtown" buildings were located near the Frisco tracks, on First Street; this street paralleled the 1882 railroad spur that was the lifeblood of early Tulsa. Merchants such as Jeff Archer built their businesses on First Street to be at the center of town, and be in a convenient location for visiting cowboys to spend their end-of-cattle-drive paychecks. The streets parallel to First Street (i.e. on a west-east axis) to the north and south were numbered sequentially: e.g. Second St. North and Second St. South were the next streets in either direction. The streets perpendicular to the Frisco tracks (i.e. on a north-south axis) began with Main Street as the starting point for the grid; the streets east of Main St. were named after cities in the eastern United States, and the

[5] James Monroe Hall, *The Beginning of Tulsa* (Tulsa, revised 1933), 6.

streets west of Main were names after western U.S. cities. The sum effect of Tulsa's early city planning was to create a passable imitation of civilization on the frontier; Tulsa's planners had great plans for the future, as seen in details like the street-grid scheme. By the 1920s, Tulsa was the self-proclaimed "Magic City" and "Oil Capital of the World." Tulsa used its oil money to embark on ambitious public and private development: skyscrapers downtown, Art Deco buildings like Boston Avenue Methodist Church, and magnificent mansions such as Waite Phillips's Italianate Villa, today's Philbrook Museum. Like Tel Aviv, Tulsa commissioned public works and private pet-projects to showcase the sophistication and modernity of the brand-new city.

Boston Avenue Methodist Church

In the 1920s-1930s, Tulsa and Tel Aviv were young cities with vast economic resources, but lacking in a clear identity; therefore, architecture, and promotion of a specific past (a myth) became essential. This myth was of the modern, an ideal contrasted against the mythic non-modern, or the "savage" or "not-civilized" native (i.e. the American Indian and the Arab). The civic promotors portrayed the city's success as down to the city's founding character types: Tulsa promoted the entrepreneur, the oilman, and the cowboy; Tel Aviv promoted the Zionist—the hard-working European-descended Jew. The celebration of these ideal types created unity and an ideal of toughness and resolve as well as ingenuity and entrepreneurial spirit; for example, the "Tulsa Spirit" which allowed the city to overcome all odds, and Zionist propaganda proclaiming Tel Aviv the "First Hebrew City" when it was only a small neighborhood just outside Jaffa. Wealth and international information networks were the keys to proclaiming the growth myths of Tulsa and Tel Aviv worldwide: Tel Aviv did this through Zionist agencies such as Keren Hayesod and Tulsa did this through international petroleum corporations and expositions.

Since the 1930s, Tulsa and Tel Aviv have continued the general trajectory outlined for their early years, but with one significant difference: the flaws in Western-style urban land-development patterns have become apparent, leading some people (e.g. civil rights leaders, environmentalists, urban theorists) to re-evaluate the promotion myths of modern cities. Tulsa and Tel Aviv have both sprawled haphazardly, but in a manner that benefits only the wealthy and the white (i.e. European ancestry). For example, in the 1970s Tulsa built taller skyscrapers, but the downtown increasingly became a "ghost town" after 5:00 pm, and commercial establishments moved southward, following middle-class whites. Black Tulsans, along with the city's heavy industry, were isolated in the northern section. Native Americans were one of many smaller minority groups marginalized from mainstream Tulsa's white neighborhoods. By the 2010s, Tulsa is more ethnically/racially integrated than before (e.g. many African Americans have moved to southern neighborhoods), there has been an influx of Hispanics, and downtown Tulsa has been renovated with public/private money (especially the Vision 2000 and Vision 2025 plans), but overall the city remains a sprawling, automobile-based city with extremely wealthy areas contrasted with much poverty. Likewise, since 1970 Tel Aviv has lost much of its regional influence to municipalities in its metropolitan region. Today, Tel Aviv is the Middle East's most expensive city to live in, is dependent on automobiles and buses, and alongside areas of enormous wealth are areas of dire poverty—especially in the southern sections (the historically Arab sections). Big plans for public parks (e.g. Tulsa's Gathering Place and Tel Aviv's Ariel Sharon Park) and new buildings are how policymakers respond. However, the lesson of modern urban history is that these sorts of large-scale, expensive projects typically do not work as planned. Urban policymakers would do well to learn the lessons of the past, beginning with a re-evaluation of standardized modern land-use patterns.

Modern, westernized cities have recurring problems--despite wealth and despite ambitious development projects--because too often people believe the founding myths: they mistake the surface facts of building a city through land use patterns and aggressive booster promotion as being true progress. But, proclaiming a city to be a success or a "light for the world" does not mean that it is a successful city. All too often, Tulsa and Tel Aviv--like many other modern cities--chose to believe the myth, and devoted their energy to supporting it. That is why, even today, Tulsa and Tel Aviv still promote their history as frontier settlements that rapidly grew into world-class cities in the early twentieth century. That is also why contemporary Tel Aviv and Tulsa face issues of image and redevelopment, directly related to the inevitable cultural conflict: the USA/Indian dialectic and the Israeli/Arab dialectic. Today, Tulsa and Tel Aviv face dilemmas because, from the beginning, their leaders emphasized ill-founded myths of western-style modernity.

The Myth of the Frontiers

The myth of the frontier was common to both Tulsa and Tel Aviv, and this was no accident: the frontier symbolized and justified American and Zionist control and takeover of the land as progress.

The concept of the frontier as an essential part of the American identity was popularized in the U.S. by Frederick Jackson Turner in 1893--that year, Turner, an ambitious young historian, publically declared that the era of the frontier in U.S. history was over. Turner defined the frontier as "the meeting place between civilization and savagery." Turner's thesis rested on a clear bias: to him, it was beyond question that European civilization had rightfully taken supremacy over natives' savagery; in short, Turner's thesis created a new booster slogan to celebrate the spread of America's European-derived culture, society, and development norms. According to Turner, the spread of the United States westward was the "the record of social evolution. It begins with the Indian and the hunter; it goes on to tell of the disintegration of savagery by the entrance of the trader, the pathfinder of civilization; we read the annals of the pastoral stage in ranch life; the exploitation of the soil by the raising of unrotated crops of corn and wheat in sparsely settled farming communities; the intensive culture of the denser farm settlement; and finally the manufacturing organization with city and factory system." Turner's description is an apt booster image of the ideology of Manifest Destiny and the triumph of the modern.[6]

---

[6] Frederick Jackson Turner, "The Significance of the Frontier in American History," 1893.

The bulk of Turner's famous, though discredited, "frontier thesis" is that the frontier was the unifying American trait: that the wilderness shaped American democracy. "The effect of the Indian frontier as a consolidating agent in our history is important." Turner explained further: "civilization in America has followed the arteries made by geology, pouring an ever richer tide through them, until at last the slender paths of aboriginal intercourse have been broadened and interwoven into the complex mazes of modern commercial lines; the wilderness has been interpenetrated by lines of civilization growing ever more numerous. It is like the steady growth of a complex nervous system for the originally simple, inert continent." The most important theme is the United States' rapid "progress from savage conditions" into a coherent and civilized nation; "to the frontier, the American intellect owes its striking characteristics" of "coarseness and strength combined with acuteness and inquisitiveness, that practical, inventive turn of mind, quick to find expedients, that masterful grasp of material things, lacking in the artistic but powerful to effect great ends, that restless, nervous energy, that dominant individualism, working for good and for evil, and withal that buoyancy and exuberance which comes with freedom." Turner's explanation for American Exceptionalism—what made the United States unique—were these "traits of the frontier, or traits called out elsewhere because of the existence of the frontier." Currently, it is out of fashion to argue in support of American Exceptionalism; Turner's thesis is really only cited as an example of a past, simpler view of the United States and of the world. Nevertheless, the sentiments Turner expressed are not so different than the patriotic grand narrative still expressed in grade-school textbooks and by politicians up for election.

The image of the frontier as the outpost of civilization also typifies the language of the Zionist movement circa 1900; for example, Theodore Herzl wrote in his pamphlet *The Jewish State* in 1896: "The Jews who wish for a State will have it. We shall live at last as free men on our own soil [in Palestine], and die peacefully in our own homes. The world will be freed by our liberty, enriched by our wealth, magnified by our greatness. And whatever we attempt there to accomplish for our own welfare, will react powerfully and beneficially for the good of humanity." Herzl saw the U.S. settlement of interior North America as a model, although he found land-runs impractical and not suitably scientific. He wrote: "In America the occupation of newly opened territory is set about in naive fashion. The settlers assemble on the frontier, and at the appointed time make a simultaneous and violent rush for their portions." Instead, Herzl proposed that for Zionist settlement in Palestine "[land] lots in provinces and towns will be sold by auction, and paid for, not with money, but in work." Centralized authorities (i.e. Herzl and the leaders of the Zionist movement) would draft the development plan for "streets, bridges, waterworks, etc., necessary for traffic." "Everything must be systematically settled beforehand [...and] Every social and technical achievement of our age… must be employed." "By these means a country [in Palestine] can be occupied and a State founded."[7]

As the examples of Turner and Herzl show, Europeans and Americans portrayed their nations' expansions as positive and inevitable, and downplayed or ignored the human cost. Put simply, Europeans preferred to downplay the status and achievements of natives in order to justify their outright takeover of already-occupied land. The rights of the natives were expressly ignored.

European Imperial networks were the basis of the clash over land in North America and Palestine. Because of the rise of European networks of exploration, colonies, and commerce in the preceding centuries (c. 1420-1800), European traders and explorers had travelled around the globe and had built up a lucrative political-economic system. Moreover, the European Enlightenment (c. 1650-1800) had increased scientific knowledge, technology, and fueled Europeans' belief that they were more advanced and civilized than natives they met up with. This became a self-fulfilling prophecy. Europeans by this time had developed a society based on permanent dwellings and communities/cities, of the importance of separating humans from nature, and private property. Neither the American Indians nor the Palestinian Arabs had systems of private land use, but of course their use of the land--for agriculture, settlements, hunting and gathering—was no less essential to their survival than to Europeans or Americans.

Natives and Europeans or Americans had very different customs. Most importantly, Native Americans did not have a similar conception of private ownership of land;

[7] Theodore Herzl, *The Jewish State*, 1896.

Europeans and Americans exploited this fact over and over again. Native Americans had a very different conception of what ownership of the land meant—thus the stories about how settlers "bought" sections of land from natives for paltry sums, and then felt aggrieved when the natives did not seem to understand settler claims to have permanent right to said land. This story was common and old by the mid-nineteenth century; a famous example of this is the Dutch "purchase" of Manhattan Island for a paltry sum. The point is that natives found the European (and later, American) concept of purchasing private land to be strange; and moreover, Europeans (and later, Americans) observed native settlements to not be "civilized" because of the lack of permanent European-style cities and socio-economic structures. As American westward expansion rapidly spread in the nineteenth century, the concept of America's Manifest Destiny, or inherent right to the land, justified wholesale appropriation of native lands, and the mass removal of native tribes. This was very much an imperialist argument and justification; Manifest Destiny was the sense of American civilization defeating savage natives, as accomplished through establishing European-style land use--e.g. settler farms, forts, and villages/cities--in areas where existing native land use had existed more seamlessly with the land.

The conflict in both North America and Palestine centered on the contested claims to the land. Zionism and Manifest Destiny were the ideologies that boosters of European-derived settlement used to promote their cause; these ideologies relied on some facts, but were primarily concerned with mobilizing settlers to not think, but act. As a result, Euro-Jewish and American settlers were dismissive of the claims to the land of the people already living on, or using the land. In the view of Native Americans and the Palestinian Arabs, the Zionist and American settlers were clearly incorrect to seize the land for themselves. The violence of the current Arab-Israeli conflict is well-known, and extraordinary. The tensions of the USA-Native American conflict are less violent, but both situations are aptly considered conflicts, with ideals, identities, and land at stake, and both conflicts still burn.

What was the claim of European-descended settlers to these lands?

The Zionist claim to the land of Palestine is complicated because Jews did live in the area during Biblical times, although they were expelled after the sack of Jerusalem by Roman General (and soon-to-be Emperor) Titus in 70 AD, which began the Jewish Diaspora; the problem was that Palestine was settled by other peoples in the interim. Over the following centuries, Palestine was controlled by a series of empires: Roman, Byzantine, and Ottoman. By the late-nineteenth century, the Arab inhabitants of Palestine had lived there for many generations. When the Zionists sought to establish their Jewish State in Palestine, it was as interlopers in collusion with the British Imperial system.

In North America, the claim is based squarely on the belief in the superior civilization of Europeans. Following the discovery of the "New World" at the end of the fifteenth century (1492), the immediate history of Europeans' interaction with natives was war, greed, and deceit. As colonies grew and flourished, the natives were pushed aside. Like their colonial forebears, Americans in the nineteenth century viewed Native Americans as an obstacle to the spread of their settlements and economic opportunities; therefore, they advocated for pro-settlement U.S. government policy to force tribes to relocate west.

In the decades after the American Revolution (1775-1783), the United States consolidated its political-economic control of the eastern states and began spreading westward. The Appalachian mountain range had been an initial barrier to westward expansion, but this had largely been conquered by the American Revolution. In 1790, European claims to western lands (France and Spain and England all claimed considerable territory) were a primary block to American expansion. The 1803 Louisiana Purchase, under President Thomas Jefferson, gave the U.S. rights (as far as the European nations were concerned) to settle much of the interior of the continent; today's state of Oklahoma was at the southern edge of this tract of land (the Red River, now the boundary between Oklahoma and Texas, was generally established as the southern edge). Native American tribes were also blocks to American expansion: the Five Civilized Tribes, located in the South, were the initial focus of U.S. policy. President Andrew Jackson's Indian Removal Act of 1830 forced these tribes—the Creek, Cherokee, Chickasaw, Seminole, and Choctaw—to relocate west to what would be termed "Indian Territory." By the late-nineteenth century (1880s-1890s), Indian Territory, present-day eastern

Oklahoma, was a prime area remaining for American settlement: railroads, to serve the cattle trade, and the discovery of oil were the economic drivers. For men like Frederick Jackson Turner, transforming Indian Territory into the State of Oklahoma was synonymous with the final triumph of civilization and the closing of the frontier.

The nineteenth century was also the period of renewed European interest in the Holy Land--especially Jerusalem--and was when European nations sought to obtain control of the Middle East: beginning with Napoleon's campaign of Egypt, siege of Jaffa, and attempt to capture Jerusalem (1798-1801). The nineteenth century period was also the twilight of the Ottoman Empire, based in Istanbul. Jaffa, the precursor to Tel Aviv, was a frontier provincial capital of the Ottoman Empire; a proud seaport city, Jaffa had previously fallen on hard times, but during this period it modernized and became internationally famous for its citrus orchards and export. Jaffa was the primary port for sea-travelers to Jerusalem. Its strategic location, yet vulnerability, as a frontier city of the vast and declining Ottoman Empire, made Jaffa and its environs a much easier target for conquest or settlement than Jerusalem. Jerusalem was the ultimate prize; Jaffa was a pragmatic foothold. European Jews were able to begin considering the possibility of relocating to Palestine in the nineteenth century because of the increasing European foothold in the vicinities of Jaffa and Jerusalem, as well as in neighboring nations like Egypt.

To the Zionist ideologues and settlers, the Jewish (re)settling of Palestine, or the Land of Israel—commonly known by Zionists as Ertz Israel (ערץ ישראל)—was a story of triumphant return, and freedom from oppression. To the Zionists, therefore, it was difficult (if not impossible) to criticize their movement to Palestine as a threat to Arab natives. The Zionist Ertz Israel was a sort of ideal society, with civilized ideas of democracy or community. This line of reasoning only intensified under the British Mandate, and has remained influential in Israeli politics up to the present day. Israelis see their outright land seizure during the 1948 War of Independence as justified in accommodating the immigration of Holocaust survivors to Israel, but to the Palestinian Arabs the war in 1948 was *Al Nakba*—"the Disaster"--and Zionism is racism. The Palestinian Arabs hate Israel in part because of the manner in which the Zionist movement took over the land. Most Israelis focus on their nation's justifications and downplay the detractions, much like how Americans do—although the specifics vary by political party in both nations.

For many Americans, understanding the situation in North America is especially complicated because the political ideals of the *Declaration of Independence* and the *Constitution* make it seem harsh to condemn the new nation as Imperialist, yet there is no denying that many American citizens—as well as the U.S. government--acted horribly toward the Native Americans. Analysis of Manifest Destiny is a way of calling attention to the popular American belief in the mid-nineteenth century that the United States was destined to control the interior of North America (including parts of Mexico), and how unsavory acts relied on the justification that European-derived civilization would triumph for the greater good. Manifest Destiny allowed Americans to deprive natives of their lands and rights, by ignoring the law at will; the history of the U.S. spread westward is the recurring story of un-heeded treaties and agreements.

In both Palestine and North America, the land use patterns of the cities of Tulsa and Tel Aviv were the means of positioning American and Zionist settlers as the chosen, civilized, people who were venturing into the frontier to serve as a "light for the world." This ideological justification, however, was only achieved by actually settling the land, and solidifying the claim to civilization by creating "modern" cities. The building of modern cities—Tel Aviv and Tulsa—that forever altered the landscape by building environments of concrete, steel, and glass, was a means of realizing the ideal in physical form.

Modern City Planning

The phrase "Post-Industrial-Revolution European-derived development patterns" is a more specific way to refer to the changes in city type that began as part of and in response to the Industrial Revolution (c. 1760), but the process of implementing and justifying these development patterns is typically called "modernization." Modernization may refer to a broad assortment of changes and beliefs, but it had a specific meaning for urban infrastructure in the late-nineteenth century: its proponents wanted to erase what they interpreted as narrow, dirty, quaint, walking-oriented cities of past centuries, and instead implement an efficient, sanitary, industrial, and commercially styled city of the future. The structural changes of the modern city included: straight and wide boulevards, which required the destruction of existing areas and winding high-density streets; technological developments, such as new building materials like steel that allowed new architectural styles such as taller multi-story apartment buildings that could, in theory, efficiently and comfortably house more people; and the building of new, showcase architectural styles to proclaim the new, contemporary fashions.

Tel Aviv postcard

Most scholars see the structural transformations of Paris carried out by Baron Georges-Eugene Haussmann and Napoleon III from the 1850s to 1870 as the model for the subsequent modernization of cities in Europe, its colonial network, and other industrialized nations like the United States. Charged with transforming Paris for Napoleon III, Haussmann manipulated Paris's political system to transform the city's infrastructure. The most essential modern feature of the changes was the unified planning and implementation of the proposed policy; and though none of the individual features were revolutionary, the overall transformation was. For example, the representations of political power through architecture were not new because Paris had been the center of power since the Romans; the long wide

Tulsa At Night postcard

boulevards continued the city's tradition since the Renaissance of preferring straight streets, and which took their modern form during the rule of Louis XIV; and many of the precedents for urban renewal and infrastructure improvements had their roots in the early 19th century. The efficient bureaucratic organization and the drastic extent and swiftness of the infrastructure changes were what marked Paris's changes as truly new. Haussmann was a superior administrator: emotionless, efficient, and a prototypical "rational" planner; his personality was pragmatic, ruthless, and unconcerned with history. As the example of Paris shows, the initial model for modernization came from the top-down vision of a powerful administrator serving an autocratic regime.

Western urban-development strategies spread world-wide during the late-nineteenth century, as cities everywhere hired or copied European city planners to rebuild their cities, as part of the regularization of city blocks and infrastructure. These styles especially spread throughout Western Europe's network of colonies, allies, and competitors. The Ottoman Empire, which controlled Palestine, and the United States of America, which sought to control as much of the North American continent as possible, both adopted these newly fashionable city-building techniques. Implementing these techniques was paramount to establishing control. Orderly street grids, sanitary sewers, fire-code compliant buildings, and beautiful vistas of grand monuments were all means of proclaiming one's attainment of ideals like progress, civilization, and showcasing the achievement of the government.

Late nineteenth-century city leaders in Western Europe and America believed that an efficient and aesthetically pleasing built environment could be created through the application of technological innovation (e.g. underground sewers), new scientific knowledge (e.g. the realization that bacteria, not miasmas, caused disease), and logical design (e.g. broad, straight streets) and the creation of public parks. Therefore, reform was a major aspect of the modernization process. Areas of cities that were overcrowded, impoverished, dirty, and full of winding streets were labeled as "blight," and areas in need of redevelopment. The desire to clean up, reform, and rebuild the large sections of cities led to a continual process of tearing down the old and rebuilding the areas in the new style.

Architecturally, the ideal modern city of the late-nineteenth century was a clean, orderly, technologically innovative, but still Classical-in-style metropolis. For nineteenth-century elites, Classical-influenced architecture connoted civilization; public buildings, such as a city hall, opera house, museum, or courthouse needed to fit specific architectural standards in order to showcase its purpose to the urban viewer. This emphasis on Classicism was also evident in the early twentieth century. City planners of the time, even when they disagreed on specific foci, such as the City Beautiful (1890s-1900s), and the City Practical (1900s-1910s) movements, still agreed that technological advances should co-exist with grandiose buildings. The stylistic switch toward High-Modern architecture, such as the Bauhaus and skyscrapers, was the work of visionary renegade architects who rejected the Classical-bent of their profession. When Manhattan embraced skyscrapers, such as the 57-floor Woolworth Building (1913), this signaled a radical break, which Tulsa emulated in the 1920s; similarly, Tel Aviv's embrace of Germany's Bauhaus-school architecture in the 1930s was a self-conscious plan to embrace cutting-edge styles.

Rothschild Boulevard, 1930s

In short, there was a revolution in architectural fashions in the early-twentieth century.

The construction of public urban parks was one of the most appealing features of modern European-style cities. These parks mimicked natural areas, and were meticulously landscaped to fit an ideal perception of how nature should be, but were highly stylized. The first of these parks was London's Hyde Park (first opened 1637), which was extensively renovated for the 1851 Great Exhibition (London's World Fair). Paris followed suit with its own large park, the Bois de Boulogne, which was completed in 1858. American cities, like New York, often looked to Western Europe for ideas on how to develop and modernize, but they were also innovating in their own way. New York City's Central Park was completed in 1857, several years after London's renovation of Hyde Park, the success of which was its impetus. Large, showcase parks celebrated the genteel, civilized side of cities: in Tulsa the best example is Woodward Park (est. 1929), which includes the acclaimed Rose Garden. The success of these showcase parks led to the construction of many smaller parks. Boulevards and parks provided a pleasant space for promenade and social gathering; affluent urbanites especially took advantage of this. Smaller parks and tree-lined boulevards (modelled after Paris boulevards) also lessened the monotony of the urban environment and provided shade for street-front cafes, which became especially popular in Tel Aviv: Rothschild Boulevard is the best example.

City planners and landscape architects viewed urban parks as a means to cure the social ills endemic to crowded, industrial, cities. Frederick Law Olmsted (the designer of New York's Central Park) argued that parks would benefit working-class families. For example, in a speech Olmsted gave in 1870 to the Lowell Institute, "Public Parks and the Enlargement of Towns," he argued the urban dwellers needed green space for public health, connection to nature, and peace of mind. Olmsted believed that individuals' contentment and adherence to morality would follow if civic officials implemented parks of good design. Having showcase parks would provide a local outlet to both rich and poor for "nature" appreciation and would cultivate the positive morality of the countryside. Despite this ideal, most cities' large showpiece parks (like Olmsted's Central Park) served primarily the affluent. The affluent classes were captivated by the concept of the "Sublime" in nature, *i.e.* the seeking of a transcendental experience through the experience of exceptional natural beauty. The Hudson River School group of painters in New York, for example, painted popular leisure vacation landmarks like Niagara Falls and mountain views from the nearby Catskills. Great artists like Thomas Cole depicted in paint America's Manifest Destiny, as the story of the rise and fall of an American civilization based on the ideals of Classical Greece and Rome.

Tulsa's Rose Garden at Woodward Park

The Sublime allowed affluent residents of modern cities to indulge a fantasy of returning to nature, but in a thoroughly civilized way.

The process of modernization, however, had several significant detractions.

First, it grew from and solidified European Imperialism—both directly and indirectly. Critiquing the dichotomy of modern versus traditional (or pre-modern) is a major theme of postcolonial scholarship. The view, in short, is that describing an area as modernized was a slippery slope toward a judgmental mindset; Europeans (and Americans) used their own presuppositions about the superiority of their cities, culture, and identity as the basis to criticize non-European--style cities and cultures as primitive and hence inferior. The judgmental aspect of this dichotomy is false, because it is based on circular reasoning: someone who believes their way to be best will be blind to other, equally valid, perspectives. Europeans also used their new taste for modernism as a justification of their self-view as civilized and their condemnation of non-European society as primitive. Tel Aviv's early history can be interpreted an example of this: British control of Palestine—the British Mandate—established after the defeat of the Ottoman Empire in World War One--directly influenced the early growth of Tel Aviv. Tel Aviv was founded in the 1870s as a suburb of European-Jewish émigrés, who purposely embraced the modern European-style as a counter to existing architectural styles in Jaffa. Soon after Tel Aviv became a city in the 1910s, its rapid construction of modernist buildings in the "White City" downtown area quickly became one of the largest concentrations of Bauhaus and/or International Style architecture in the world. Tulsa's early street-grid system and skyscrapers also fit this trend, as examples of speculators presenting the as-yet-tiny settlement as an important city.

Second, modernization's connection with industrialization increased pollution and encouraged the exploitation of nature as nothing more than a set of resources. Nature, for modernized cities, was no longer seen as an organic whole but as a source of natural resources and a depository for waste.[8] Some policymakers were aware of this problem in the early twentieth century—President Theodore Roosevelt, for example, worked for

[8] Carolyn Merchant's book *The Death of Nature* (Harper and Row, 1980) offers a philosophical analysis of Europe's switch from an organic to a mechanical to an exploitative relationship with nature.

conservation and wise use of natural resources—but it was not yet a major political issue, and did not become one until circa 1960. Both Tulsa and Tel Aviv have faced significant issues with pollution.

Third, modernization necessitated the destruction of existing areas, homes, and buildings. The impoverished bore the brunt of the housing demolitions—and history-minded individuals lamented the destruction of grand old buildings. This list serves, not necessarily as a condemnation, but a reminder that specific policy and economic choices were the driving forces behind the creation of the dominant type of modernized urban infrastructure such as Tulsa and Tel Aviv both have. The new cities erased nearly all traces of the preexisting landscape.

Fourth, the separation of the white European from the "other" races was essential to the construction of national identity, where race was defined primarily by what it was not—i.e. being white because not native. This notion of race required the colonized "other" as the point of reference. Whites often arrived at the frontier with preconceived notions of the natives, and were unwilling to adapt their views even when faced with hard evidence. Both American and Zionist settlers saw European-derived civilization as representing progress and native customs (whether Native American or Arabic) as representing superstition and "darkness." The point is that the colonial system solidified the settlers' belief that their values were inherently superior to the native "other," and hence justified the belief in Zionism and Manifest Destiny.

Fifth, Modernist Architecture and city planning went to extreme lengths to achieve technological efficiency, social order, and government control through urban design. Even the most revolutionary designs had a pragmatic rationale, and are best described as unsentimental and highly logical, because they were so focused on efficiency. Modernist architects and planners often disregarded existing development or geography; for example, Le Corbusier's 1922 "Contemporary City for Three Million People" shocked his contemporaries with its unsentimental attitude of embracing the future by explicitly ignoring the past, as in razing central Paris to accommodate high-rise apartments for *Plan Voisin* (1925). Le Corbusier's plans included high-rise buildings and public green areas, much like in many public-housing projects built later in the United States. In the case of public housing, these green spaces failed as a design feature: they were deserted and often dangerous areas. The highly logical ideals of modernist architecture and planning often did not materialize as expected in reality.

Sixth, at essence, the modern is just one style among others: and preferences for tastes and styles change. An irony of the modernization process is that today, in the 21st century, compact, walkable, "quaint" cities such as were common pre-1850 are once again a popular trend: people will now pay big money to live in pre-modernized areas of cities--such as the popularity and high price-tag of Old City Jaffa in Tel Aviv, and current projects underway to build "urban" residences (that seek to replicate the feel of brownstones found in older cities like New York) in or near downtown Tulsa. In light of this, it is unwise to associate any one style of architecture or urban development as *a priori* better than another; underneath the grand rhetoric, architecture and urban development patterns merely reflect the current styles and fashions.

Deconstructing the Modern

Analyzing two cities—Tel Aviv and Tulsa—at the forefront of modern city building in areas considered frontier circa 1900 is a means of analyzing the ideologies, symbols, and ultimately the foundation of modernity itself. Tel Aviv and Tulsa are to some degree unique or unusual, but not totally. Their histories, successful booster promotion, and ongoing conflicts about the political-economic-racial/ethnic inequalities inherent to modernity provide a special perspective and allow us to step outside our typically uncritical view of the modern/contemporary built environment and, for a moment, see with a fresh perspective.

The post-modernist geographer Edward Soja argued that Los Angeles is the model for the city of the future; and the African Studies urban scholar Garth Meyers argued instead that

Tel Aviv's Modernist-Style Buildings

Lusaka, Zambia may be more accurate.[9] Without disagreeing with them (because they were discussing different analytical questions), I would like to co-opt their question and pose whether Tel Aviv and Tulsa are the model, or archetypical types, of the "Modern City."

The boosters of early Tulsa and Tel Aviv portrayed their city as archetypically modern, but with such fervor and force that it underlies their insecurity: circa 1920 Tel Aviv and Tulsa could in no way compete with Europe or the United States' great cities. Boosters could loudly compare Tel Aviv with Paris or New York or Tulsa with Chicago, but that did not make it so.

What I am suggesting is that the insecurity of Tulsa and Tel Aviv was in fact normal for self-consciously modern cities. In order to self-define their city as modern, boosters had to convince themselves that it was true; ideologies, symbols, and sleight of hand were the means. Even the most progressive modernizing cities like Paris, London, Berlin, and New York were at best a jumbled mix of newly rebuilt areas and very old areas. Affluent New Yorkers continually looked to Europe for the latest fashions and trends; London and Paris and Berlin all competed for status amongst the others to show each was more magnificent and more advanced. World's Fairs are probably the best example of this trend: any city that wanted to matter held a World Fair at some point from 1850 to 1970. Actual status did not matter although wealth did: Chicago's 1893 Columbian Exposition is a case in point. Chicago had vast railroad networks, was the center of the

---

[9] See Garth Meyers, "What if the postmetropolis is Lusaka," *African Cities: Alternative Visions of Urban Theory and Pratice* (New York: Zed Books, 2011), 21-42.

slaughterhouse and meat market, and dominated the Western markets; however, Chicago in 1893 lacked style or architectural identity and in 1871 its downtown center had been destroyed by fire. Unrelated to the lavish Fair, Chicago turned to skyscrapers (thanks to local architect Louis Sullivan) and developed its own modern style, rivaled only by New York City (the city that Chicago strove to emulate and compared itself against). Chicago was the city that Tulsa's early boosters targeted as the initial location for their promotion campaign: the 1905 Booster Train that, apocryphally at least, greatly impressed Chicago's Commercial Club. The recurring narrative is that insecurity about one's city's state of development or status caused boosters to advocate copying the latest trends (skyscrapers for the United States and International Style or Bauhaus style buildings for Europe) in order to promote that the hoped-for level of modernity had in fact been reached.

Tulsa's Modernist-Style Buildings

Most residents of Tulsa and Tel Aviv (like people in most modern cities) do not think much about their environment or why their city grew in the way it did--they either believe the officially sanctioned myth or take the everyday aspects of their life for granted or as *a priori* normal. However, there is nothing normal or inevitable about city growth, planning, or land-development patterns, just as it is incorrect to say that it was inevitable or normal for European-descended settlers to develop large cities in frontier areas that they did not clearly control. There are specific historical reasons why, and specific ideologies that explain and interpret such history, and uncovering and presenting those aspects is a major theme of this book.

Modernist development is ubiquitous today, so much so that we do not even think about it, but it was a revolution. Since circa 1760, nearly everything about land-use patterns has changed, because of features like rapidly increasing urbanization, the harnessing and abusing of the natural environment and resources, and new mass-produced goods.

Currently, much of the Earth is developed (or at least partially developed) according to European-derived modern ideals of land use: streets built on a grid system to accommodate automobiles, permanent buildings (often designed to fit specific building codes), zoning to separate various land uses, and widespread use of technology and relatively new sanitary systems (underground sewers, incinerators or landfills, running water). As a result, we as a society take the modern/contemporary built environment (i.e. the buildings, trees, streets, grass, stores, and homes of a typical city or town) for granted as *a priori* normal. Therefore, we are unable to analyze our modern built environment and development patterns from a non-biased perspective. As a consequence, we too easily accept the booster narrative of equating progress with technology and European-derived permanent settlement patterns.

Post-colonial scholarship provides a window, or a crack, that may allow us to step outside our uncritical acceptance of the modern as normal; post-colonial theory describes the conception of modernity as the interplay of imperialism, capitalism, and nationalism, which quite often derived from European-focused ideas of land-development patterns. The concept of the modern as the achievement of civilization through means of technological progress and efficient organization (often through powerful government) placed the European at the pinnacle and non-European as the savage (and the frontier as somewhere between these two poles). Post-colonial scholarship is helpful because it debunks simple notions that the facets of European political-economic and cultural control were unquestionably good. The re-writing process inherent in recent post-colonial history also pokes many holes in the trope that natives were helpless victims against the more-advanced Europeans.

However, the point I wish to make here at the outset is not the typical post-colonial argument that non-Europeans (like the Ottomans in Jaffa) were "just as modern" as the

Europeans and were modernizing on their own, but rather on the opposite spectrum (a point more common in environmentalist scholarship): natives had centuries-old practices which were in many ways more effective for their specific lands and specific climates, and it is incorrect to state that European-derived settlement was in any way an improvement. Various forms of this argument have proliferated since the late-1980s as themes like "sustainable development" and "zero waste" have become common on the global stage (e.g. promoted through the UN). A clear example of this perspective is *Mannahatta* by Eric Sanderson, which reconstructs what New York City's Manhattan Island probably looked like in 1609 when the first European explorer arrived, and uses said ecological and anthropological information about the natural ecosystems and the Lenape tribe to make an argument advocating more "sustainable" future land use policies.[10] Environmentally minded scholars are beginning to argue that Native Americans' ecologically sensitive land-use strategies were superior to European-derived land-use patterns of totally obliterating landscapes in order to build human-centered environments of concrete, wood, glass, and steel.

Native American Statue, Philbrook

[10] See Eric Sanderson, *Mannahatta: A Natural History of New York City* (New York: Abrams, 2009).

Most of us living normally affluent lives (i.e. who don't in a shantytown or favela, of which there are many still in existence), I suspect, would find it difficult to imagine living in a non-modern manner; we are dependent on our "convenient" modern lifestyles; we cannot imagine what it would be like to live without running water, permanent dwellings with air conditioning or central heat, without automobiles or airplanes, and without flush toilets, TVs, cell phones, the Internet, and rudimentary waste-disposal systems. The accounts of comparably recent urban history tell stories of the horrible smells that were commonplace in city neighborhoods (e.g., sewage ran in a crack built in the center of the street for the purpose) as well as income-blind diseases like Cholera that decimated whole populations due (we now know) to contaminated water supply. So yes, we have much better sanitary standards and conveniences today than the conditions endured by humanity in the past. But is that the only aspect that matters?

Independence Park, north-western Tel Aviv

To take seriously either the postcolonial argument or the environmentalist view is to step outside the dominant paradigm of defining the modern as equal to progress, and to begin to free ourselves from our preconceptions just enough to see outside the limits of our permanent homes with running water, or past the distaste of noxious smells and fear of disease, and seek to understand the past on its own terms and not as a straight or predestined line up to the present and an even more progressive future. This perspective is important, even as an intellectual exercise, because it allows us to consider the perspective of the native, for whom the imposition of European conceptions of private ownership of land meant the permanent loss of one's homeland. It is necessary to consider that there were potential alternative paths besides the triumph of the European-derived modern at any cost.

The histories, ideologies, symbolisms, and development patterns of Tulsa and Tel Aviv provide a unique insight into understanding the grip that the modern has had on western society since the Industrial Revolution. We take our modern human-constructed environments for granted today, but that complacency blinds us to the very real alternatives that existed. A cultural analysis of Tel Aviv and Tulsa, taking seriously the alternative routes hidden in booster propaganda, opens up enough cracks in the narrative of the modern for us to see with fresh eyes—that is the primary theme of this book.

Chapter Two

History

Tulsa and Tel Aviv

Building Tulsa and Tel Aviv according to the latest European and American standards of urban planning and architecture was an attempt at literally making the modern myth a reality. The best way to begin deconstructing a myth is to examine its factual foundations; that is the topic of this chapter.

Tulsa

Indian Territory, or present-day Oklahoma, is an area of climactic and geographical diversity: it is impossible to describe the area in a simplified manner. Tulsa, however, is in the north-eastern section, where the foothills of the Ozarks (and related mountain ranges) give way to lush forests and prairie. The area of Tulsa is a river plain adjacent to the southern-bend of the Arkansas River, with high river-ridges that mimic mountain foothills common.

The indigenous peoples in the area were of the Plains cultural grouping, although various tribes crisscrossed the area. Northeastern Oklahoma (where Tulsa is) was—at the time of first European contact--near the edge of the territory of the Siouan-Catawaba peoples from further north and the territory of the Kiowa-Tonoan peoples. A cultural grouping is a means researchers use to classify tribes based on "environmental and cultural characteristics" instead of linguistic features.[11] The Plains tribes in Oklahoma at the time of initial European contact exhibited the cultural characteristics of: hunting bison; a military society living in bands that often formed raiding and hunting parties; residing in

[11] Wendell H. Oswalt, *This Land Was Theirs: A Study of Native Americans,* Seventh Edition (Boston: McGraw-Hill Mayfield, 2001), 20-22.

temporary homes like teepees instead of permanent villages; and engaging in ceremonies with spiritual or ritual meaning.[12]

It is a common myth that American settlers chose not to settle Oklahoma (after the Louisiana Purchase) because the land was harsh and inhospitable. This myth does not apply to the Tulsa area, but rather to the western part of the state. European-descended American settlers judged the land based on its capacity for commercial activities like farming; much of the Great Plains area of present-day western Oklahoma was deemed unsuitable for farming, and so became popularly known as "The Great American Desert." These western parts—beginning in the central Cross Timbers region and extending westward to dryer areas—were the area of the famous Land Runs of the late-nineteenth century. In Oklahoma, many popular stories perpetuate the importance of the land runs (e.g. the Boomers, the Sooners), but these events did not include the Tulsa area.

Instead, the Tulsa region circa 1832 was covered with "noble groves and forests which skirt and intersect the prairies, and extend along the alluvial bottoms of the rivers" and in "these beautiful regions… the rich pasturage of the prairies is calculated to sustain herds of cattle as countless as the sands upon the sea-shore, while the flowers with which they are enameled render them a very paradise."[13]

When the author Washington Irving travelled through the would-be area of Tulsa in 1832 he found a "frontier" area to be sure, but not an uninhabited wilderness. Like most white American visitors to the area (which would soon thereafter become Indian Territory after the forced removal of the Five Civilized Tribes), Irving began his journey at Fort Gibson, the newly established U.S. Army fort (est. 1824) and gateway for American control of the region until 1888. Irving journeyed northward parallel to the Arkansas River toward the bend in the river by present-day Tulsa, where he met up with his U.S. Army Rangers escort. In his journal, which he published soon after completing the journey, Irving recorded his observations of the area. October 11 was the day on which Irving and his party paralleled the Arkansas River and camped near the site of today's Tulsa. His

---

[12] Ibid. 24-25.
[13] Washington Irving, *A Tour on the Prairies*, 1835. Full text available online: https://books.google.com/books/about/A_Tour_on_the_Prairies.html?id=fHwOAAAAQAAJ

perceptions quoted here reflect what we might expect most new-arrivals to have thought. About the area south of Tulsa Irving said:

> We travelled slowly, and made a considerable halt at noon. After resuming our march, we came in sight of the Arkansas. It presented a broad and rapid stream, bordered by a beach of fine sand, overgrown with Willows and cotton-wood trees. Beyond the river, the eye wandered over a beautiful champaign country, of flowery plains and sloping uplands, diversified by groves and clumps of trees, and long screens of woodland; *the whole wearing the aspect of complete, and even ornamental cultivation, instead of native wilderness* [emphasis added]. Not far from the river, on an open eminence, we passed through the recently deserted camping place of an Osage war party. The frames of the tents or wigwams remained, consisting of poles bent into an arch, with each end stuck into the ground: these are intertwined with twigs and branches, and covered with bark and skins…[we saw] in the present skeleton camp, the wigwam in which the chiefs had held their consultations around the council-fire; and an open area, well trampled down, on which the grand war-dance had been performed.[14]

The important features of this quote, besides the general description of the area, is that Irving clearly describes the land as cultivated and as inhabited; this description would seem to go against the (commonly argued by American settlers) view that the area was wilderness and virtually uninhabited (because the natives didn't count in their estimation).

About the actual area that would become Tulsa Irving had similar things to say. On October 12, Irving described the area as "overshadowed by lofty trees, with straight, smooth trunks, like stately columns; and as the glancing rays of the sun shone through the transparent leaves, tinted with the many-colored hues of autumn [I realized]…there is a

[14] Ibid.

grandeur and solemnity in our spacious forests of the West."[15] Irving says "our forests" because of the Louisiana Purchase, and in his account he takes obvious pride in the freshness and vigor of the area—which is not surprising for an East-Coast writer recently returned from Europe, and on a spur-of-the moment adventure in the interior of North America. Irving continued: we came "upon the banks of the Arkansas, at a place where tracks of numerous horses, all entering the water, showed where a party of Osage hunters had recently crossed the river on their way to the buffalo range"; "A little farther on, we reached a straggling Osage village on the banks of the Arkansas."[16]

The first recorded permanent settlement at the site of Tulsa was established in 1836 by a band of Creeks who had been forced to relocate to Indian Territory. This group, known as the Lochapoka Creeks, because such was the name of their original home settlement in Alabama, recreated their hometown near the banks of the Arkansas River by a large Oak Tree known as the Council Oak. The name Tulsa was an Anglicized version of the Creek word for town or city: Tulsi. The Lochapoka had carried the ashes of their hometown with them on their journey to Indian Territory, and upon choosing the site of their new village near the banks of the Arkansas River, ritually combined these ashes with their new Council Fire to mark continuity. Therefore, "from the ashes of a council fire in a small Creek Indian village [in Alabama] in the new land grew a place called Tulsa."[17]

The Council Oak

The chief of the Lochapoka Creeks, who established the first recorded town-site at Tulsa in 1836, was Opothle Yahola. Achee Yahola was the next chief, he was a "revered

[15] Ibid.

[16] Ibid.

[17] William Butler, *Tulsa 75: A History of Tulsa* (Tulsa: The Metropolitan Tulsa Chamber of Commerce, 1975), 19.

figure" who "led and preserved the Lochapoka as a people" until he died during a smallpox epidemic in 1850.[18] During the Civil War, Tulsee Fixico assumed control.

The Lochapoka were not unique among the variants of the Five Civilized Tribes in choosing to live in the eastern half of Indian Territory. Many other displaced Indian communities settled in the area of eastern Oklahoma, not far from the Lochapoka. Around "seventy thousand square miles" were available for settlement, but the Civilized Tribes generally remained in the eastern portion of Indian Territory because the climate in the east was similar to that of their homelands (e.g. Alabama, Georgia, Mississippi, and Florida) and they feared raids by Plains tribes who already claimed the western area, regardless of new U.S. treaties. The climate of the eastern section "was temperate and humid, with a long growing season and short, mild winters" and the terrain was also "comforting to the refugees" because the mixed-prairie forests offered protection as well as memories of the natural environment of their former homes.[19]

The Civilized Tribes, including the Creeks, prospered from the 1830s until the 1860s, when the Civil War began. All these tribes lived up to their civilized epithet by developing complex and flourishing systems of settlement, society, and trade. The tribe owned lands in common and strictly prohibited persons from outside the tribe to purchase or occupy tribal-controlled land. To get around this rule, white men would marry into the tribe, and mixed-blood individuals were able to flourish under tribal law. Moreover, slavery was legal, and many of the wealthy tribesmen established slave-owning plantations to rival the states of the U.S. South. Other signs of civilization were many. Steamboats travelled up and down the shallow rivers—like the Arkansas River—to bring farm equipment, fine household goods like china and linens, and other essential goods to the tribal settlements in exchange for raw materials like furs, cotton, and corn. Regular mail service also existed along the twelve stations of the Butterfield Stage route in eastern Indian Territory. The Civilized Tribes all had written constitutions (except the Seminoles). They also boasted orderly school systems for children and youths

---

[18] Danney Goble, *Tulsa!*, 26.
[19] H. Wayne Morgan and Anne Hodges Morgan, *Oklahoma: A History* (New York: W.W. Norton & Company, 1977; revised 1984), 28-29.

as well as colleges for women and men; the children of the Civilized Tribes were "better educated and more concerned about learning than were their white counterparts on the frontier."[20]

One of Tulsa's most important families, the Perrymans, moved to Tulsa at this time. In 1848 Lewis Perryman, a Creek, opened a trading post along the Arkansas River (near today's 31st St. and Riverside Dr., where the Gathering Place park project is under construction). This trading post thrived, because "Indian customers came on foot, pony, or by canoe to exchange their wild turkey, venison, pelts and pecans for calico, sugar, coffee and farm implements."[21] The Perrymans were a prominent mixed-Creek family (European, African, Native American in heritage), but they were not part of the Lochapoka group; the Perrymans were outsiders, who had voluntarily moved into the area of Fort Gibson and the Three Forks (the center of U.S. presence in Indian Territory) in the 1820s. As was common for affluent Creeks, the Perrymans owned black slaves to work their commercial-use farmland.

Fort Gibson

The Lochapoka Creeks' settlement, like many Native American settlements in Indian Territory, was disrupted during the U.S. Civil War (1861-1865). Native American tribes were split in allegiance for the Confederacy and the Union. The result was much in-fighting and wholesale destruction. The existing communities and settlements of Indian Territory were stalled or devastated by the war. By 1864, most of the Creek Nation had been overrun by solders from both the Union and the Confederacy. The Lochapoka settlement at Tulsa

[20] Ibid. 29-31.
[21] William Butler, *Tulsa 75*, 23-25.

had been largely destroyed during the Civil War. "All the public buildings and homes of the Lochapoka had been destroyed, all livestock had been stolen. The town was deserted and overgrown with weeds." "But the Lochapokas came back to their town and began a second settlement of Tulsa." George B. Perryman, one of Lewis Perryman's sons, returned to the family's Tulsa home and built a ranch that was, when completed, "the largest in the Creek Nation."[22] The Lochapoka who survived the war, however, rebuilt their settlement in a different way: "Rather than cluster their homes nearby, the people tended to scatter across the surrounding area" and "each dwelling lay near a little patch of corn enclosed by the owner's rail fence."[23]

After the war, the U.S. government punished the tribes as Confederates, regardless of the side specific individuals had supported. In 1866, the U.S. government revised its treaties with the Five Civilized Tribes and forced them to cede portions of their land. The effects and implementation of these new treaties varied among the tribes. From 1866 to the 1880s, Indian Territory became the repository for Native American tribes forced to relocate from all over the U.S.; the Five Civilized Tribes were forced to give up their lands in order to accommodate the newcomers. By the 1880s, white settlers had set their hearts on settling land in Indian Territory; hence the opening up of new American towns and cities like Tulsa and Muskogee along newly built railroads, and the commencing of land runs in the central and western parts of the territory.

In this period after the end of the Civil War, the Perryman family increased its prominence in the Tulsa area. None of the official histories of Tulsa explain in detail what happened to the Lochapoka, and instead focus on the spread of American settlers and infrastructure in to the area; the Perryman family is the clearest link cited between the Creek settlement of Tulsa and the later American settlement of the same name.

Josiah Perryman became Tulsa's first postmaster in 1879 when the U.S. government constructed an official post office in Tulsa. Tulsa's new post office was the main place to send or receive mail for the entire region. Soon after the founding of the post office,

---

[22] Ibid. 27.

[23] Danney Goble, *Tulsa!*, 29-30.

Tulsa's first school, the Creek Nation School, opened with an initial enrollment of 36 students.[24] The new post office and school helped make Tulsa important regionally.

1n the 1870s, many more whites began to settle and establish homesteads along on Creek land, in present-day Tulsa. The Creeks had laxer policies than the nearby Cherokees regarding non-tribal men settling land; the Creeks wanted payment in return for allowing the use of their lands. Some of these American settlers, like Chauncey A. Owen, married into the Creeks and so had legal rights to own land. Many others, such as Antoine Gillis, resorted to squatting on the land, openly defying the Creeks, because they refused to buy the required annual permits from the Creeks.[25]

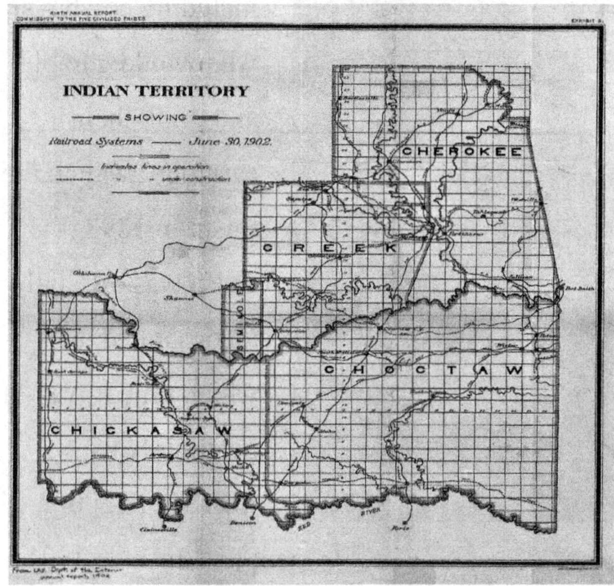

Railroads in Indian Territory, 1902

The year 1882 is the official date of Tulsa's founding, because that was the date of the construction of the Frisco railroad spur west of Vinita toward the Arkansas River. Choosing 1882 as the founding date of Tulsa fit well with the American narrative at any rate.

J.M. Hall opened Tulsa's first store building in 1882 on the west side of Main and Frisco: the J.M. Hall Co. & Store.[26] Also in 1882, George and John Bullette opened Tulsa's first general store along the Frisco railroad line in what would soon be Tulsa's downtown (1st St. and Boulder St.). Strip-mining for coal began in Tulsa in 1882 (and would remain a constant in Tulsa until 1955).[27]

[24] Ibid. 27.
[25] Ibid. 30.
[26] Clarence Douglas, *The History of Tulsa* (Chicago: S.J. Clark Publishing Company, 1921), 135.
[27] "Nature Labored at Length," *Tulsa Tribune,* October 17, 1973.

In the next few decades, the economy boomed because of the cattle trade, the railroad, and merchants setting up business. Permanent buildings began to be commonplace: churches, schools, hotels, and comfortable houses. Many of these original settlers were of mixed-native and white heritage. Nevertheless, Indian Territory was a place where Anglo-American riff-raff hid from the authorities. Tulsa had its share of outlaws, and unsavory types: including cowboys who would gamble and drink their earnings away in the town. In 1898, Tulsa was officially incorporated, at which time it was "a bustling 'cow town'" of 1200 people.[28] In June 1901, oil was discovered nearby at Red Fork, only five miles away from downtown Tulsa; J.C.W. Bland and Fred S. Clinton drilled this first oil and gas well on the homestead of Sue Bland. Fred Clinton later wrote:

Tulsa, 1894

> Our decision to drill here was based upon our faith in the development of [petroleum] resources of the Indian Territory, the industrial activity and oil interests in Kansas and Texas, the allotment of Indian lands, and the establishing of the legal right of ownership of property which presented a golden opportunity for immediate progress if we could strike oil and secure national publicity without delay. We had no lease or leases when we decided to make a try by leaps and bounds for instant national publicity. *This was the first oil and gas discovery well in the Indian Territory, now Oklahoma, which was nationally publicized,* resulting in

[28] *Visit Oklahoma: Travel Stamp Album and Guide Book* (Oklahoma City, OK: Oklahoma Planning and Resources Board, 1952), 14.

> the rapid industrial development of Tulsa and Oklahoma, and finally to establishing Tulsa as the Oil Capital of the World...
>
> God supplies resources. Man develops them. Men build cities.[29]

The discovery of oil in 1905 at the nearby Kiefer-Glenn Pool furthered the opportunity for Tulsa's sustained growth and transformation into a city. The oil pools were not in Tulsa proper, but enterprising merchants in Tulsa worked to facilitate the new City of Tulsa as the administrative center of the oil boom. For this purpose, enterprising Tulsans built hotels, stores, lodging for oil workers, entertainment venues, and business space (which included the lobbies of the hotels), and just as importantly they successfully lobbied three more railroads (for a total of four) to pass through Tulsa. Due to this foresight, Tulsa-based petroleum companies were able to quickly get to later oil fields, like the massive Cushing-Drumright field discovered in 1912, establish wells there, and further the economic growth of Tulsa. The Cushing-Drumright field was then the largest oil field in existence, and it produced 236 million barrels between 1912 and 1919; although this oil field furthered the growth of established nearby towns like Cushing and spawned boom towns like Markham and Oilton, Tulsa was a primary benefactor of the field, as the most established companies and geologists were based there.[30] Tulsa was also a petroleum-processing center. By 1919 there were two refineries, both located across the Arkansas River from downtown: the Texaco and the Cosden refineries. Joshua Cosden's refinery was, in 1919, the largest independent oil refinery in the world.

Frisco RR Bridge and Wagon Bridge over the Arkansas River, 1909

[29] Fred S. Clinton, "The Beginning of the International Petroleum Exposition and Congress," *The Chronicles of Oklahoma* 26 (Winter 1948–49), 479.

[30] Oklahoma Historical Society, "Cushing-Drumright Field," Web. Accessed November 21, 2016. http://www.okhistory.org/publications/enc/entry.php?entry=CU008

Bird's-Eye View of Tulsa, 1918

From 1915 through 1930, Tulsa experienced a new growth spurt due to the next wave of oil discovery nearby. World War One (1914-1919) significantly increased demand for U.S. oil, and Tulsa benefitted—Tulsa virtually cornered the oil market at a time when, due to the war, both demand and prices for oil were exceptionally high. The 1912 discovery of the huge Cushing Field jumpstarted oil-related industries in Tulsa; that same year huge international companies like Royal Dutch-Shell entered the U.S. market (in cooperation with American Gasoline Co.) and began "marketing imported gasoline in California and Roxana Petroleum Co. in Tulsa for exploration and production" and Harry F. Sinclair began his oil-production company in Tulsa: Sinclair Oil Co. In 1915, the State of Oklahoma enacted its first market-demand proration law and the well-established Carter Oil Co. set up a new division in Tulsa. In 1917, the Mid-Continent Oil & Gas Association formed, when a group of influential oil men gathered at the Hotel Tulsa in downtown and agreed to work together, in order to efficiently deliver petroleum to the Allied war effort; in 1919, Tulsa became the regional headquarters of this association, under the leadership of local oilmen including Frank Phillips (of nearby Bartlesville) and William G. ("Bill") Skelly.

Tulsa's great wealth, due to the beginning of the oil boom to the late 1920s, meant that many of "the great names in petroleum resided in the city" such as "notables" like Joshua Cosden, Waite Phillips, Jean Paul Getty, Harry Sinclair, William "Bill" Skelly, and Thomas Gilcrease.[31] These influential oilmen and entrepreneurs combined with bankers like J.M. Hall to make up Tulsa's elite.

Cosden Refinery, c. 1921

Tulsa's wealthy boosters were determined to have their efforts be recorded for posterity. Ranging from stunts like the 1905 Booster Train tour to a dress showcased at the 1896 Civic Parade comprised of one hundred dollar bills, Tulsa's boosters sought to showcase the city's "spirit" and wealth by any means. Founders like J.M. Hall wrote autobiographical histories of their version of Tulsa's early days: Hall's book, *The Beginning of Tulsa,* was first published in 1927 and revised in 1933. Likewise, in a 1921 promotional book of the city, author Clarence Douglas recorded the city's early historical events in order for "future historians to bring their work up to 1920" and thus ensure the perpetuation of 1920-booster interpretations of Tulsa "that might otherwise be lost." Paramount was showing that Tulsa was a city with depth and high-culture and not a mere flash-in-the-pan oil town full of bumpkins. Douglas's history of Tulsa was published in 1921—when Tulsa was in the midst of oil wealth and civic promotion—so emphasized that "men of national and international reputation visiting Tulsa have expressed their wonder and astonishment, at its type and its unique construction, and by most visitors it has been described as a city with a distinct personality." As examples, the list included political, military, and figures of note after World War One. "General John J. Pershing called Tulsa the wonder city of the world. Ex-President William Taft named it Marvelous Tulsa. Senator James Hamilton Lewis called

[31] Carl E. Gregory, "Tulsa," The Encyclopedia of Oklahoma History and Culture, www.okhistory.org. Accessed November 2016.

Tulsa the Miracle City and Madame Schumann-Heink described it as The City Beautiful. Baron Rosen of Belgium designated Tulsa the City Magnificent, and by Theodore Roosevelt it was termed the Magic City."[32]

Tulsa Race Riot, 1921

Aftermath of the Race Riot, 1921

Despite appearances, all was not perfect in early Tulsa. In fact, Tulsa was a city divided by race and class, and fueled by competition. In 1921 the city boosters of Tulsa were vocally celebrating their promotional myth of Tulsa as "The Magic City" and the new "Oil Capital of the World," but this year was also the year of Oklahoma's bloodiest racial violence: the Tulsa Race Riot. Prior to the race riot, the flourishing African-American area of Greenwood was commonly known as "Black Wall Street" and it was one of the most significant and flourishing African American communities in the United States.

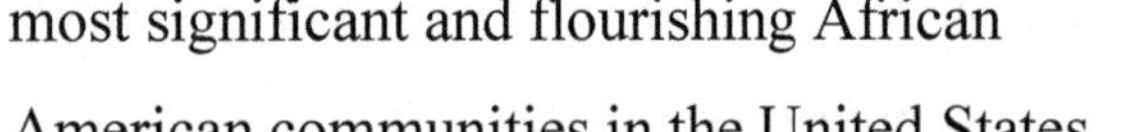

The Race Riot occurred between May 31 and June 1 and destroyed nearly forty city blocks in the African-American areas north of downtown. The area destroyed included Black Wall Street—today commemorated near Greenwood and Archer—and although Tulsa's African-American neighborhoods rebounded, the riot's impact was devastating.

[32] Clarence Douglas, *The History of Tulsa* (Chicago: S.J. Clark Publishing Company, 1921), 5.

Beginning in 1923, Tulsa hosted its first International Petroleum Exposition (IPE). As described by an oilman, Fred Clinton, "The sponsors and supporters of the International Petroleum Exposition and Congress sought and secured a useful, self-supporting commercial commodity—petroleum—older than civilization and wide as the world, as the object of civic consideration." Moreover, "Petroleum, or earth oil, the magic fluid known from time immemorial, has been transformed into myriad uses by the ingenuity of modern man." Tulsa's rapid growth and wealth are because "Practically every human activity of today is dependent upon earth oil." Earl Sneed, a Tulsa attorney, was the first man to suggest publically the idea for the Exposition, saying it would be like a World's Fair, which "with all its side show features would give thrills to the young people, knowledge to the oil fraternity, opportunity to make world-wide acquaintance, renew friendships, and firmly establish Tulsa for all time as the oil center of the entire world."[33]

Oil Field near Tulsa, c. 1921

The 1923 exposition was held downtown from Main to Cheyenne streets and from Archer to Cameron streets. "With the exception of 1926 the IPE was held annually from 1923 through 1930 for a week to ten days during October and grew in attendance from a few thousand to more than 120,000. As it was the premier show of its kind, various petroleum-related organizations, such as the Mid-Continent Oil and Gas Association and the American Petroleum Institute, scheduled their meetings in Tulsa during the exposition." The highlight was when "Pres. Calvin Coolidge opened the 1927 exposition from the White House by pressing a button that caused a simulated gusher to blow wild on the IPE grounds." Despite the Great Depression, the IPE was held in 1930, 1934, 1936, 1938, and 1940.[34]

[33] Fred S. Clinton, "The Beginning of the International Petroleum Exposition and Congress," 480.

[34] Bobby D. Weaver, "International Petroleum Exposition," *The Encyclopedia of Oklahoma History and Culture*, www.okhistory.org. Accessed November 2016.

By the 1920s-1930s, Tulsa was the self-proclaimed "Magic City" and "Oil Capital of the World" and boasted a collection of cutting-edge Art Deco buildings and skyscrapers as well as luxurious or extravagant private mansions. Tulsa's Art Deco, skyscrapers, villas, new middle-class homes, were intended to signify wealth and sophistication. During these decades, Tulsa grew exponentially due to its vast economic resources. The city's elite set about creating an image of high culture based on the ideals of the American Dream: individual hard work, entrepreneurship, and belief in progress. Tulsans looked to civic ideals as a means of creating unity and celebrating Tulsans' toughness, ingenuity and entrepreneurial spirit: the "Tulsa Spirit." Tulsa's Commercial Club promoted the Tulsa Spirit as the city's "Can Do Attitude" as the reason for its existence and rapid success. Tulsa's vast oil wealth was the key to proclaiming the booster myths worldwide: Tulsa did this through its annual International Petroleum Exposition.

Tulsa Mansions, 1921

Incredibly wealthy oilmen and their families dominated early Tulsa politics and society. These oil-rich elites built huge mansions in competition with other, but also sponsored public buildings and organizations. "Oil millionaires used their money in diverse ways" and created "a tradition of civic pride and a desire for public decoration…unequaled in the rest of the state." Multi-millionaires were common, and many of this Tulsa elite sought to establish claims to the type of high-society found in well-established cities like New York or Chicago, and establish a philanthropic tradition.[35]

The skyscraper became the trademark symbol of downtown Tulsa, as it was for many other American cities. The architectural style of the skyscraper, or a multi-story building that was roughly ten stories or higher, was first developed by Chicago-based architect Louis Sullivan in 1891 (e.g. the Wainwright Building in St. Louis), and quickly morphed

[35] H. Wayne Morgan and Anne Hodges Morgan, *Oklahoma: A History,* 159.

into taller and more striking examples. Tulsa's early skyscrapers included: the 16-story Cosden Building, completed in 1918; the 24-story Philtower, 1928; the 22-story and 400-foot tall National Bank of Tulsa Building (now 3200 South Boston Building) from 1928; and the 225-foot tall (equivalent to about 20 stories) Boston Avenue Methodist Church, completed in 1929.

National Bank of Tulsa Building

In Tulsa, the Art Deco style in particular took hold: this style originated in France in the 1910s and became very popular in the 1920a and 1930s; Tulsa was growing rapidly during these decades, and its oil-rich patrons could afford to indulge in the latest *avant-garde* architectural fashions. The Art Deco style clearly celebrated modernism, or the colorfully expressive exuberance and energy of industrial society. Tulsa's *nouveau riche* elite wanted nothing more than to be taken seriously as knowledgeable consumers of high culture and arts: Tulsa's Art Deco buildings made this case for them.

During the Great Depression, poverty and economic depression was widespread, and the "Okies" (such as the fictional Joad family portrayed by John Steinbeck in his famous 1939 novel *The Grapes of Wrath*) were a widespread symbol of the worst poverty. In much of Oklahoma, the oil bust of 1930 led to economic problems, and the Dust Bowl decimated agriculture across the state; however, Tulsa was relatively untouched by the worst problems of the Great Depression. This was because Tulsa had diversified beyond its origins as a banking and oil city. The huge economic gains of Tulsa's oil companies did subside during the 1930s—and so the IPE was not held every year—but its oil firms remained solvent.

In the 1940s through 1960s Tulsa grew especially to the south, which was where the city's white, affluent population was concentrated: the industry was concentrated in the less-affluent and/or African American area north of downtown. The city grew in racially segregated terms: more growth in white, affluent areas, to the south and east of downtown, yet from 1940 to 1950, Tulsa's population grew by more than 40,000 persons, to reach a 1950 total of 182,740. In 1960, Tulsa had 258,271 inhabitants. Tulsa continued to develop new infrastructure and industry; Tulsa was now a corporate center, due to relocation of industry from the northeast, and an aerospace center, in addition to an important oil city and railroad hub. Tulsa's monumental architecture, including its many skyscrapers, was a statement of the city's progressive intentions.

The main difference in Tulsa's skyscrapers of this postwar period, contrasted with those of the 1920s, was that the new buildings and office complexes were located alongside expressways on the periphery, instead of downtown. These office complexes—as was common in U.S. cities—were huge buildings on large campuses: they did not replicate the dense fabric of the downtown. By the 1950s, expressways crisscrossed the city, enabling easier transportation from the periphery to the downtown—and vice versa. Across the United States, suburbanization exploded after the end of World War Two, as returning veterans and their families sought to move into single-family homes. In Tulsa, the most popular area for middle-class whites was the area south of downtown.

Visit Oklahoma! 1952

In most respects, Tulsa was a typical American city at this time. As a "Sunbelt" city--the scholarly term for cities in the U.S. South and West that benefitted from industrial relocation from the U.S. North and Upper Midwest or "Rustbelt"--Tulsa flourished economically. It remained a petroleum center, but diversified to include other industries, becoming, for example, an aerospace and medical center. During the 1950s and 1960s, many U.S. companies opened regional offices in Tulsa, which brought many white-collar executives and blue-collar workers to the city from elsewhere. "A principal center for manufacturing of oil industry equipment, Tulsa's manufacturing does not rest solely on the oil industry, however, and nearly half of the 635 manufacturing plants now produce for a diversified market." Moreover, Tulsa "is an important operations center for five major airlines and four railroads" as well as a regional center for wholesale and retail markets."[36]

During the postwar economic boom of the 1950s and 1960s, The International Petroleum Exposition continued to symbolize Tulsa's distinctive place in the global oil industry. To maximize profits, "the exposition's board of directors voted to hold it every five years in a number of buildings on twenty-plus acres at the fair grounds" and "the venue continued to draw in excess of three hundred thousand visitors." In 1966, the IPE attracted its largest number of visitors ever: for that year's event all the older buildings were demolished and replaced by a ten-acre exhibition hall; in 1966, Tulsa's distinctive Golden Driller statue was commissioned by the Mid-Continent Supply Company to adorn the entrance to the exhibition.[37]

In 1952, the Oklahoma Planning and Resources Board described Tulsa as follows:

> …long known as 'the Oil Capital of the World,' [Tulsa] is one of the Southwest's most beautiful and progressive metropolitan centers… The story of Tulsa is literally the story of oil in the Southwest…the Oil Capital is headquarters for more than 700 oil producing, refining, transporting, marketing, or special service companies in the petroleum industry. Tulsa is the world's purchasing market and is the control center for much of the oil exploration and development in not only the Southwest and Midwest areas, but also Canada, Latin and South America, and the Middle East.
>
> Tulsa is the home of the International Petroleum Exposition—the largest exhibit of any such industry. Resumed in 1948 following World War II, the Exposition attracted 301,000 visitors.[38]

[36] *Visit Oklahoma,* 14.
[37] Bobby D. Weaver, "International Petroleum Exposition," Accessed November 2016.
[38] *Visit Oklahoma,* 14.

Economic success brought striving for high-culture. Architecturally, in 1952, boosters promoted Tulsa as "nationally-known" for "its beautiful churches" including the Art Deco Boston Avenue Methodist Church and the Gothic-style First Methodist Church. The mansions and artwork collections of Tulsa's golden-era tycoons such as Waite Phillips and Thomas Gilcrease had been converted into museums. By the 1950s, Philbrook Art Center and the Gilcrease Foundation had nationally significant collections of American Indian and Southwestern Art, as well as extensive research libraries. Tulsa was also well-known for its symphony orchestra, and had organized a civic opera club in the hope of establishing a permanent year-round organization.[39]

By 1970, 330,350 people lived in Tulsa, and the city was flourishing; yet, harsh times were on the horizon. The fortunes and fate of the IPE, as before, symbolized Tulsa's as a whole. Unfortunately, the collapse of the oil market in the 1970s, amid economic chaos and new competition from Houston's oil industries, led to disappointing IPE events in 1976 and 1979. The IPE was overwhelmed with these difficulties "due to competition from other such events, plus logistical and financial difficulties."[40] The final straw was absolutely dismal attendance at the 1979 IPE, which forced the directors to cancel the event permanently.

Since the 1970s, Tulsa has sprawled outwardly, especially toward the south and east, following the "white flight" patterns of the hollowing out of the central city in favor of the growth of the suburbs. In the 1970s, Tulsa built taller skyscrapers, topped off with the 52-story One Williams Tower (1975), which is now known as the BOK Tower, but the downtown increasingly fell into disuse and disrepair; it was a "ghost town" after 5:00pm, with few apartments, restaurants, or commercial establishments to attract people there. Racially and ethnically, Tulsa's

Central Tulsa, c. 2000

[39] Ibid 14-5.

[40] Bobby D. Weaver, "International Petroleum Exposition," Accessed November 2016.

neighborhoods are becoming more mixed then in previous decades. In 2000 Tulsa had 393,049 residents within city limits. Its population had grown despite the fact that its many suburbs, such as Broken Arrow, Jenks, Owasso, Bixby, and Sapulpa were growing at a faster rate.

By 2016, Tulsa is the second-largest city in Oklahoma with a little under half a million residents (403, 505) and one of the largest metropolitan areas in the region, with nearly one million people (905,755) and over a quarter of Oklahoma's total population. Tulsa is more ethnically/racially integrated than before (e.g. many blacks have moved to southern neighborhoods), there has been an influx of Hispanics, and downtown Tulsa has been renovated with public/private money to attract upscale apartments and dining and entertainment venues, but overall the city remains a sprawling, automobile-based, city with extremely wealthy areas and very poor areas.

Tel Aviv

The area of Palestine, or present-day Israel, is a Mediterranean climate with warm summers and temperate winters. Tel Aviv is located on the flat coastal plain, with sand dunes intermixed with fertile land suitable for large-scale orchards as well as agricultural cultivation. The early Zionist settlers often claimed the area was a backwater, a place in disrepair, because that fit their narrative of the area as an abandoned place that would flourish under their possession of the region.

In the nineteenth century, European and American travelers developed renewed interest in Palestine, and Jaffa was a primary port of entry for visitors headed to Jerusalem. Many of these visitors were Christian, and they often published travelogue accounts of the region: many of them, as wealthy "civilized" individuals, expressed very similar deprecatory sentiments about Palestine as did the Zionists. Jaffa Port is an ancient seaport, with a rocky entrance, and it is not capable of receiving large vessels; instead, large ships anchor off shore and passengers must reach shore by means of small landing craft. As described by an American visitor in the 1830s: "The harbor of Jaffa is not good, or rather there is no harbor worthy of the name." To the Euro-American visitor, the city of Jaffa circa 1839 was more impressive as a small, ancient, "Oriental" city. "Jaffa stands on a sandy point, which projects a little distance into the sea. The ground at the point is more elevated than farther back. It is a walled town, with a double wall and fosse in some places; all, however, much out of repair." "Most of the houses have a very old appearance; few of them are good; the streets are narrow, crooked and filthy, as in almost all the Turkish towns." "The houses are much crowded together, and cover a very small space, considering their number." Jaffa "has also, in the noble plain of Sharon, a most admirable back country," which circa 1839 just outside of city limits had "gardens, enclosed lots and fields, many of them filled with trees, as fig, orange, lemon, pomegranate, palm." "There is much sand in the district that borders the coast, and in many places directly on the coast the sand has fairly taken possession—nothing is seen but fields of white sand."[41]

Jaffa at the beginning of the twentieth century was majority Arab, but cosmopolitan, and was an important city at the edges of the Istanbul-based Ottoman Empire. The Ottomans had a complex system of laws, which prevented non-native Jews from immigrating to Palestine and purchasing land; when Zionist Jews began ignoring or transgressing these laws, local Arabs grew frustrated and saw the Jews increasingly as a threat. Nevertheless, Jewish immigrants from Europe were often able to find individuals willing to sell unpalatable land: such as marshes to drain.[42]

Jaffa's Orchards, late-19th C.

[41] Rev. J.D. Paxton, *Letters on Palestine and Egypt Written During Two Years Residence* (Lexington, KY: A.T. Skillman), 126-129.

The eventual city of Tel Aviv began as a loose network of Jewish neighborhoods in the 1880s, adjacent to Jaffa. Neve Shalom was the first land-area purchased by the Zionists in 1884, and was settled in 1890; Neve Tzedek (נווה צדק) was the first Zionist neighborhood settled in the (later) area of Tel Aviv: purchased in 1886, it was settled in 1887.[43] In 1891-92 the Ottoman government built a railway station in this neighborhood of Jaffa, to serve as the terminus of the railroad line to Jerusalem. This station, known in Hebrew as the HaTachana railroad station, served Jaffa, but was built at the northern limits of that city, at the edge of the neighborhood of Manshiya (מנשייה) and bordering on the early Jewish neighborhoods of Neve Tzedek and Neve Shalom.[44] Manshiya was built in the 19th century, along a majestic beach. Manshiya was a mixed neighborhood, with both Arabs and Jews. The Hassan Bek mosque (מסגד חסן בק), built in 1916, was at the forefront of the land-struggle symbolized by Manshiya. Hassan Bek (also known as Hassan Bey) was the Ottoman governor of Jaffa from 1914-1916. As part of his strategy to limit the spread of Jewish land-holdings and town-building in the Jaffa area, Hassan Bek decided to build a new, prominent Mosque well to the north of central Jaffa. This stratagem did keep the spread of Tel Aviv from encroaching too quickly on central Jaffa, but ultimately failed; in the decades of the British Mandate this neighborhood marked the dividing line between Jaffa and Tel Aviv.

Members of Ahuzat Bayit

Despite Zionist rhetoric, the Ottomans had begun the modernization of Jaffa—using French ideas as a model—in the late-nineteenth century and until their defeat in World War One. It is a mistake to believe the myth perpetuated by the Zionist

---

42 Martin Gilbert, *Israel: A History*, (New York: Harper Perennial, 2008), 30.

43 Mark LeVine, *Overthrowing Geography*, 63, 76.

44 Sharon Rotbard, *White City, Black City: Architecture and War in Tel Aviv and Jaffa* (Cambridge, MA: The MIT Press, 2015), 72.

leaders of Tel Aviv that Jaffa was only an ancient, backwater, town that was rightfully subsumed by Tel Aviv. By the official date of Tel Aviv's establishment in 1909, Jaffa's leaders had, in fact, built modern-style public monuments, such as the Clock Tower (1900-1903) to commemorate the reign of Abd al-Hamid II, the Ottoman Sultan from 1876-1909.

The official founding of Tel Aviv is commonly dated to April 11, 1909, when the Ahuzat Bayit society held a lottery to allocate newly purchased plots of land to the sixty-six Jewish families who gathered on the sand dunes north of Jaffa. Tel Aviv's first mayor, Meir Dizengoff, was a member of the society. The founder of the Ahuzat Bayit Society was a watchmaker, Akiva Aryeh Weiss; Weiss encouraged other Zionists to form a "Hebrew City" based on the principles of Ebenezer Howard's Garden City ideal then in vogue in Western Europe; the ideal Garden City was in fact anti-urban, and closer to a group of suburbs linked together by rail. The financial backing for the Society's purchase of the plot of land that would become Tel Aviv's historical center was provided by a wealthy Jewish-Dutch banker, Jacobus Kann; Kann was able to legally purchase and register the land in his name because he was a Dutch citizen.[45] The lottery format to divide the land among the members of Ahuzat Bayit was: Weiss gathered 120 seashells, 60 of which were white and 60 were grey; each member's name was written on a white shell and a specific plot of land was written on each grey shell. The plots were thus selected by drawing one white shell and one grey shell at a time to match a family or individual with a plot of land.

In the first decade after Tel Aviv's founding, Zionist leaders perceived the neighborhood as an uniquely urban Hebrew settlement destined to become the symbolic beacon of the Zionist state. Tel Aviv's founders envisioned it as "a place where purity and cleanliness will reign." This attitude pervaded the "mythic" ideal of Tel Aviv, where mundane events took on symbolic importance.[46] Tel Aviv soon combined with the earlier Jewish neighborhoods, including Neve Tzedek in 1913. One of the main factors in Tel Aviv's rapid growth into a city with high population density and high land values was land

[45] "Jacobus Street, Corner of Oblivion," *Ha'areetz,* April 01, 2009.
[46] Maoz Azaryahu,, "Tel Aviv: Mythography of a City" (Syracuse: Syracuse University Press, 2016), 37.

speculation, due in large part to the scramble of European-descended Jews to relocate there. Tel Aviv's settlement was part the Second Aliyah of Jewish immigration, mostly from Eastern Europe (1904-1914). Theodore Herzl's rhetoric promoting Zionism convinced many well-off European Jews to finance and support Jewish immigration to Ottoman-controlled Palestine, even though said immigration was not permitted under Ottoman law.

Typically, the Zionist ideal was of the rural communal settlement: the *kibbutz* (קיבוץ); in Tel Aviv, the ideal of the communal settlement merged with ideals of replicating Europe's great cities in Palestine. Even though Tel Aviv quickly outgrew the size of the *kibbutzim* (קיבוצים), it kept many of the ideological aspects of Zionism: attachment to the land of Palestine and settling it in a scientific, European-derived way. The boosters of Tel Aviv promoted their vision of progress based on Zionist ideals of hard work and enterprise, but with European/American ideals of the modern as the height of human civilization. Wealth was the key to proclaiming the myths worldwide: Tel Aviv did this through Zionist agencies such as Keren Hayesod and the Jewish National Fund, which sought wealthy international donors to aid the Zionist cause.

The British assumed control of Palestine after the defeat of the Ottoman Empire in World War One (1917). The French took the northern part, including Syria, and the British took the southern part, including the area of present-day Israel. The British Mandate was never an official colony, but it was certainly part of British Imperial ambitions. After the Ottoman Empire's defeat in 1918, the British Mandate government allowed both Arabs and Jews to own land; however, the British unsuccessfully sought to appease local Arabs by implementing immigration quotas on Jews into Palestine.

Tel Aviv flourished under the British-Mandate government in the 1920s and 1930s, and during those years it developed ambitious plans to model and compete with European cities; Jaffa was always the rival that Tel Aviv sought to overcome. In 1922, Jaffa was clearly superior to Tel Aviv, in that it had 47,709 residents: 20,699 Muslim, 20,152 Jewish, and 6850 Christian. However, Tel Aviv was growing, and already had 15,185 residents, of which 15,065 were Jews, 78 were Muslim, and 42 were Christian.[47] The British Mandate built Tel Aviv's own railway station in 1920, the Tel Aviv Custom House Station, located in the heart of Tel Aviv at Rehov Yehuda Halevi and Rehov HaRakevet (i.e. Railway Street), next to the newly built Customs House.

The Zionists brought European ideas about development with them to Palestine. European planning theory, such as Ebenezer Howard's Garden City plans, formed a basis for early Tel Aviv, and the municipality employed a British architect, Patrick Geddes, to draft its ambitious (but not ratified) plan in 1925. Tel Aviv by the mid-1930s had abandoned its original Mediterranean-themed buildings and adopted modernist architecture as its style of choice; Bauhaus and International Style are the two terms commonly used to describe Tel Aviv's defining architectural style. Tel Aviv grew rapidly in the north and east, away from the more Arab and more impoverished area of Jaffa. Tel Aviv almost exclusively commissioned modernist architecture, and as in other European-colonial cities in the Middle East and Africa the widespread use of modernist architecture was in fact a statement of the city's progressive European basis (as opposed to the trope of the "traditional"). Modernist architecture was more common in colonial settings than in Europe proper because of a colony's assumed *tabula rasa* for development and unequal power structures. The architecture, combined with growth patterns of these cities (more growth in white, affluent areas), clearly illustrated the scheme of promoting new money wealth/affluence and the latest trends of European culture and society.

Allenby St., 1930s

[47] *Palestine: Report and General Abstracts of the Census of 1922*, complied by J.B. Barron, 6

In the 1920s-1930s, Tel Aviv was a young city with vast economic resources, but lacking in a clear identity; therefore, architecture, and promotion of a specific booster myth became essential. This myth was of the "modern," an ideal contrasted against the "non-modern" indigenous peoples: Tel Aviv promoted the Zionist, the hard-working European-descended Jew. The portrayal of Tel Aviv as the quintessential Zionist City created unity and an ideal of toughness and hard work as well as ingenuity and entrepreneurial spirit. In order to accomplish this dream, the Zionists focused not only on architecture, but also on education and the Hebrew language. Hebrew was the ancient Jewish language, the holy language of the *Torah*, but it had fallen out of use and was no longer spoken by the late-nineteenth century: Eliezer Ben Yehuda revitalized Hebrew by developing dictionaries of the language and coining new words "according to the rules of grammar and linguistic analogy from Semitic roots: Aramaic and especially from Arabic roots" that filled in "the deficiencies of the Hebrew language" enough to enable its everyday use.[48]

Many Zionists saw the spoken and written use of the Hebrew language in the everyday as vital to the success and symbolism of the Zionist identity. Using Hebrew would allow all Jews in Palestine, regardless of the nation from which they emigrated, to speak a common language and build a common identity. The essential step was to educate children and new arrivals in the use of the Hebrew language. In October 1925, the municipality of Tel Aviv introduced a compulsory school system. With this system, Tel Aviv became "the first city in modern Jewish Palestine to introduce" such a school system, which was "modelled after the ancient system of the High Priest Joshua Ben Gamala" from the Second Temple period in Jerusalem.[49] Joshua died circa 69/70 C.E., just prior to the Roman sack of Jerusalem; the ancient system Joshua developed was "a universal system of education after all previous attempts failed. He evolved a system whereby 'teachers of young children be appointed in each district and each town,' whereas previously they were to be found only in Jerusalem. In addition he laid down

[48] Joshua Blau, *The Renaissance of Modern Hebrew and Modern Standard Arabic* (Berkeley, California: University of California Press. 1981), 33.
[49] "Tel Aviv Introduces Compulsory Public School System," *The Sentinel*, October 30, 1925, page 2.

sound pedagogical principles."[50] In 1925, on the occasion of this new compulsory school--in line with traditional Jewish ways—the Tel Aviv municipality declared its decision was a "drastic change in the Tel Aviv educational system," and that "No child is to be rejected from the Hebrew school, irrespective of his parents to pay the tuition fee." Prior to 1925, all Jewish schools in Tel Aviv were funded and run by the Zionist Executive; these schools fit into Zionism as a means of teaching the Hebrew language to complement the other aspects of Zionist culture and thought imparted to the young generation. Under the post-1925 arrangement, the Zionist Executive would contribute 8,000 pounds annually and roughly 12,000 pounds from tuition charged to parents.[51]

British Mandate authorities were keenly aware of the tensions between Arab and Jew in Palestine, for example in the conflict between Jaffa and Tel Aviv: Arabs and Jews commonly fought over population counts and quotas. The 1931 Census was a case in point; Tel Aviv was included as part of the District of Jaffa, because the census defined towns "as units under the jurisdiction of a municipal council and included the town of Tel Aviv which is under the jurisdiction of a local council invested with wide municipal powers." Nevertheless, the British-Mandate officials understood that "It will not be difficult for those who are interested in Greater Jerusalem, Greater Jaffa, Greater Tel Aviv or Greater Haifa to arrange the given statistics to suit their own purposes."[52] In 1931, Tel Aviv had 46,101 persons: 45,564 Jews, 106 Muslims, 143 Christians; and a total of 12,545 occupied houses. That year, Jaffa was roughly the same size, with 51,866 inhabitants (35,506 Muslim, 7209 Jew, 9132 Christian) and 11,304 occupied houses.[53] British concerns about the political conflict between Arab Jaffa and Jewish Tel Aviv were justified. Tel Aviv elites were competitive about outdoing Jaffa; they sought to improve public perceptions about Tel Aviv at the expense of Jaffa. For example, facts cited in press releases reported in the *Palestine Bulletin* about Tel Aviv in 1931 were wide-ranging. Then, Tel Aviv had "more than 170 physicians in the town," who were

---

[50] "Joshua Ben Gamela," Jewish Virtual Library, Accessed December 2016. https://www.jewishvirtuallibrary.org/jsource/judaica/ejud_0002_0011_0_10355.html

[51] *The Sentinel*, October 30, 1925, page 2.

[52] *Census of Palestine 1931, Population of Villages, Towns, and Administrative Areas,* complied by E. Mills (Jerusalem: 1932), iii.

[53] *Census of Palestine 1931,* 13-15.

"spreading unemployment among the unqualified doctors of Jaffa";[54] this quote is meaningful because in 1931 Jaffa was still the major urban center for most services. In 1934 work began on a new hospital in Tel Aviv and it opened in 1936; this hospital, commissioned by the main Zionist trade union, the Histadrut (הסתדרות) and in particular the Kupat Cholim (קופת חולים) Worker's Sick Fund, was located on the Tel Aviv-Petah Tikvah Road and had "60 beds and will also have a special maternity ward of twenty four beds." This building was designed by Arieh Sharon (אריה שרון), a young architect from Tel Aviv fresh from graduating from the Bauhaus School in Dessau Germany, who would go on to become the most prolific of the Israeli architects affiliated with the Bauhaus School.[55] This hospital's opening in 1936 meant that "Tel Aviv's mounting population of Jews" "was jubilant" because they would no longer have "to rely on the Government Hospital in the Arab city of Jaffa hitherto."[56]

The 1930s were tumultuous. Tel Aviv had long been one of the major ports-of-entry to Israel, and so the metropolitan area was an initial refuge for many immigrants. Cheap housing, basic sanitation, and also makeshift refugee camps, or ma'barot (מעברות), were common in the area. Moreover, conflict between Arab and Jew led to violent confrontation between Arabs in Jaffa and Jews in Tel Aviv. Violence and strikes at Jaffa Port, as well as the desire for economic growth, led to Tel Aviv constructing its own port in 1936-1938; the mayor during this period (1936-1953) was Israel Rokach, a staunch Zionist. Arabs in Jaffa became frustrated about the competition posed by Tel Aviv Port and reacted violently, which led to British support for Tel Aviv against Jaffa in this instance: the British bombed part of the old-city section of Jaffa as a punishment. By 1939, concurrent with the outbreak of war in Europe, Tel Aviv had 160,000 inhabitants. The immigration levels had skyrocketed in the wake of Nazi Germany's persecution of Jews, and because of tensions in Europe on the eve of World War Two. In 1939, Tel Aviv had roughly 30 percent of all Jews living in Palestine.

---

[54] *The Palestine Bulletin*, March 02, 1931, page 5.
[55] "Histadruth To Open Tel Aviv Hospital," *The Sentinel*, October 18, 1934, page 21.
[56] "Tel Aviv to Have Hospital For Contagious Diseases," *The Sentinel*, August 06, 1936.

Jaffa Port, 1930s

By the mid-1940s, Tel Aviv was eclipsing Jaffa on nearly every level as the major urban center of the region. One of the most important symbolic projects to showcase Tel Aviv's eclipse of Jaffa was the seaside park in northern Tel Aviv now called Independence Park. In March 1946, the Tel Aviv municipality expropriated 17 dunams (4.2 acres) of land that had formerly been "the Moslem cemetery here" and began building a 102-dunam (25-acre) sea-front park that "will be the largest in Palestine" and cover "the dunes along the coast south of Tel Aviv Port.[57] Further south along the coast, closer to Jaffa, the neighborhood of Manshiya continued to be at the forefront of friction between Arab and Jew. By 1945, at the end of World War Two but before the post-Holocaust immigration surge, Tel Aviv had 222,000 inhabitants. In 1945, faced with the reality of post-war emigration from Europe, the Tel Aviv Municipality began a program to find lodgings for newly arrived refugees, announcing that "People living in large flats will be asked to volunteer accommodations for refugees for a period of six to nine months until the present housing shortage is relaxed."[58]

[57] "102 Dunam Park for Tel Aviv," *The Palestine Post,* March 20, 1946, page 3.
[58] "Housing for Refugees in Tel Aviv," *The Palestine Post,* April 30, 1945, page 3.

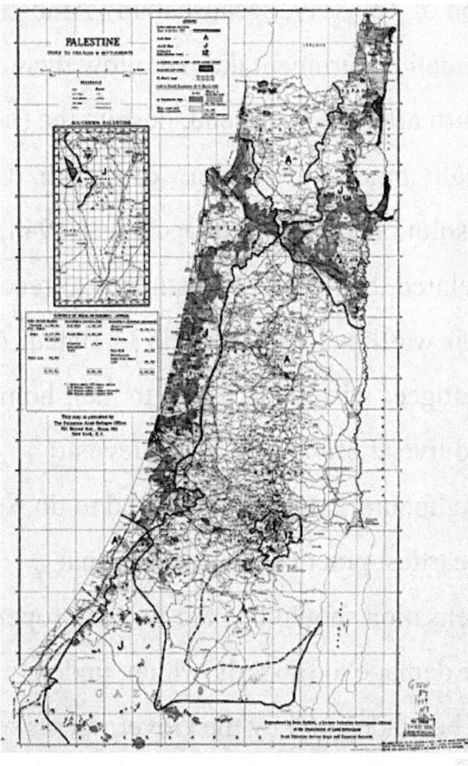

Palestinian Villages, c. 1948

The British withdrew from Palestine soon after World War Two, because of tensions with both Jews and Arabs in Palestine, and Britain's lack of desire to maintain its Imperial holdings after 1945. The British Mandate ended on May 14, 1948, and the British ceded the question of who should control Palestine to the UN for deliberation. Jewish nationalists did not wait for the UN, but seized the opportunity to establish a Jewish State. In 1948 the Jews launched a war of independence and quickly defeated the Arab forces; at this point most Arabs abandoned their villages, but Arabs in cities like Haifa and Jaffa were more likely to stay (at least at first).

The 1948 War of Independence (May 15 through March 1949) completed Tel Aviv's eclipse of Jaffa. During the War of Independence there were snipers from rooftops in the Arab neighborhoods--including from the minaret of the Hassan Bek mosque--onto the streets of Tel Aviv-Jaffa, causing loss of life. Due to the perceived threat to Tel Aviv posed by Arabs in Manshiya, the Irgun (i.e. Jewish Liberation or Resistance fighters) decided to conquer the neighborhood. During the fighting that ensued, the Irgun's tactics included the planned destruction of many houses and infrastructure in the neighborhood; the Irgun also broadcast radio propaganda in Arabic, to frighten and intimidate the Arab civilian population.[59]

[59] Sharon Rotbard, *White City, Black City,* 98-108.

The 1948 war profoundly changed the population of Tel Aviv, because many Arabs fled their homes to avoid the fighting, but the new Israeli government did not allow them to return after the war's end, despite the (non-legally binding) UN's Law of Return. UN Resolution 194, passed December 1948, declared the right of Palestinians to recoup their wartime losses; Article 11 stated: Arab "refugees wishing to return to their homes and live at peace with their [Jewish] neighbours should be permitted to do so at the earliest practicable date, and that compensation should be paid for the property of those choosing not to return and for loss of or damage to property which, under principles of international law or equity, should be made good by the Governments or authorities responsible."[60] In the 1948 War, Israel did not capture central Jerusalem, but only the Western outskirts; West Jerusalem, built in a modern style somewhat similar to Tel Aviv, is the site of the Knesset and most of Israel's government buildings. In 1950 the unified metropolis of Tel Aviv-Yafo was created.

Manshiya in Ruins, 1948

The unification of Jaffa and Tel Aviv after the 1948 War of Independence presented a more-complex face to the city's development. Tel Aviv's White City downtown area, which is famous for its modernist architecture, remained the focal point. The city also enjoyed flourishing nightlife and a commercial network ranging from coffee shops to beachfront resorts. Behind the vibrant exterior, several environmental and planning questions concerned local policymakers. The metropolis was growing exponentially due to large-scale immigration after Israel opened its borders to all Jews. Sprawling developments, like affluent northern Tel Aviv, threatened to lessen the pull of the downtown. The architecture and street layout of Jaffa, which is a compact, ancient seaport, contradicted the modern image that Tel Aviv's boosters wished to sell. Keeping

[60] United Nations General Assembly, 194 (III). Palestine -- Progress Report of the United Nations, December 1948.

the city clean, as in managing litter and visible dirt, was another challenge. Due to factors such as these, infrastructure concerns were top priority for city officials.

After the 1948 War, the Manshiya area became a place for impoverished immigrants. Because it, like many of the earlier Jewish neighborhoods like Neve Tzedek and Neve Shalom, were becoming "slum" areas, Israeli city planners in the 1950s and 1960s debated proposals to rebuild the area. Ultimately, in 1963 city officials decided to raze Manshiya and some of nearby Neve Tzedek. With the demolition of the area's buildings, huge amounts of rubble were stored on the nearby beach, and because the cost of removal of debris was very high, it was cheaper to cover it over with earth and build a park. Thus most of the Manshiya area became the expansive open area of Charles Clore Park that still functions as a geographical divisor between Tel Aviv and Old City Jaffa. Today, only two historical buildings from Manshiya remain; the Hassan Bek mosque is one, and the other is an old Palestinian house that has been renovated into the foundation of the Etzl Museum of Independence in Charles Clore Park. Charles Clore Park's expansive emptiness underlies the obvious erasure of Manshiya's past; the ruins of the Dolphinarium, where a Hamas suicide-bomber blew himself up in a crowed discotheque in 2001, makes the charged atmosphere of the seaside park even stranger since the Tel Aviv municipality has not as yet demolished or renovated the ruin.[61]

Dolphinarum's ruins, 2014

Tel Aviv grew steadily from 1948 through the mid-1960s. This growth was at the expense of Arab Jaffa: in 1947 Jaffa had 85,000 inhabitants, mostly Arab; at the end of the 1948 War of Israeli Independence, Jaffa had only 4500 Arabs left. In 1948 Tel Aviv had 248,000 persons; in 1951, after merging with Jaffa, it had 345,000. The growth of the

[61] For details on the planning debate over the Dolphinarium site, see "Tel Aviv Postpones Demolition of Abandoned Dolphinarium," *Ha'aretz,* March 8, 2012.

city of Tel Aviv peaked in the 1960s: the 1961 population was 386,100 and in 1964 it was 394,000 inhabitants. Tel Aviv-Yafo municipal policymakers' mindset in the 1950s and 1960s was finding a way to accommodate rapid growth in the most sanitary and efficient way possible.

Since 1970 Tel Aviv has lost much of its regional influence to municipalities in its metropolitan region. After Tel Aviv peaked in size in 1964 (394,000 persons) it experienced a decline, relative to its immediate suburbs, which continued to expand. This was because of factors like the reduced birthrate and slow-rise trend of mortality (ageing population) in the central city, and emigration of people from the city's core to the suburbs or to elsewhere in Israel. In 1969 Tel Aviv had 390,000 inhabitants, and municipal officials had not yet realized that the city had already reached its zenith. That year, the Tel Aviv-Yafo municipality commissioned a long-term plan for growth, "Planning For The Future": this plan was for the year 2000 to accommodate 600,000 inhabitants, as part of a Greater Tel Aviv of a million and a half. Tel Aviv-Yafo's planners understood their miscalculation by the late 1970s, and revised their plans. In 1969, Tel Aviv had 237,000 workers—and 31% of all of Israel's industrial workers. In 1969 there were 261,000 houses (of all sizes) and the plan was to increase that number to 650,000 by 2000.[62]

During this period the surrounding municipalities rapidly gained population: these areas' population increased by 104% from 1961 through 1976. Tel Aviv-Yafo had 48% of the metropolitan-region's total population in 1961, 33% in 1972, and 29% in 1976. By 1976 the geographic pattern of the core-city of Tel Aviv-Yafo and the outer-circle settlements was clearly evident in the metropolitan area. In 1961 the metro region had 804,375 persons (the suburbs already outnumbered the city with 418,275 persons as compared to the city's 386,100). By 1972 the total had risen to 1,102,273 (suburbs 840,248 as compared with 363,750 in the city) and in 1977 it was 1,183,448 (840,248 in the suburbs compared to the city's 343,200)—and the discrepancy between suburb and city continued

[62] Moshe Goldstein, *Breve Historia de Tel-Aviv*, Biblioteca Popular Judia, (Buenos Aires: Congreso Judio Mundial), 1969.

to rise in the following years.[63] Despite the suburbs' rapid growth, Tel Aviv-Yafo remained administratively independent--except for the Dan Region Association of Towns--but was "an integral part of the vast metropolis."[64]

Central Tel Aviv, 2014

The 1970s and 1980s marked the time when Israel unabashedly became a consumer nation, and the Tel Aviv metropolitan area—as Israel's major economic, artistic, and industrial metropolis--remained the epicenter of this trend. Tel Aviv had embraced Western-style commercialism before the rest of Israel; in the 1950s and 1960s, for example, Tel Aviv's left-leaning *Ha'aretz* (הארץ) newspaper ran many advertisements for consumer goods, including women's and men's fashion, automobiles, and various foods and beverages.[65] Part of the reason for the increased commercialism of the 1970s and 1980s was Israel's alliance with the United States after the 1967 war, and declining support for the (socialist-inspired) Labor government was further eroded by the perceived debacle of the 1973 October (Yom Kippur) War; the (far-right) Likud party had already been gaining prominence before 1973, but Likud officially won control of the Israeli government in the 1977 elections.[66]

---

[63] Tel Aviv-Yafo Municipality, *The Population of T.A.-Yafo in the 1970s Development and Trends,* November 1978.

[64] The Dan Region Association of Towns (created 1966) coordinates policymaking to address the infrastructure challenges created by the metropolitan region's urban sprawl. Tel Aviv-Yafo Municipality, *The Population of T.A.-Yafo in the 1970s Development and Trends,* November 1978. See also "Municipality Council requires the Dan Cities Association," *Davar*, July 12, 1966.

[65] These, and many similar advertisements, were common in the Ha'areetz (Hebrew-language) daily newspapers from 1950-1969.

[66] For an analysis of how this political switch affected Israeli commercialism and environmentalism, see Orr Karassin, "The Battle of the 'True Believers': Environmentalism in Israeli Party Politics" from *Between Ruin and Restoration: An Environmental History of Israel*, edited by Daniel Orenstein, Alon Tal, and Char Miller (Pittsburg: University of Pittsburg Press, 2013), 168-189.

Skyscrapers, both office buildings and high-rise hotels, have become fashionable in Tel Aviv since the 1970s. Hotels have long flanked the seaside; for example, in 1973 environmentalists argued that Tel Aviv was "beginning to develop its own 'micro-climate' due mainly to the city's large hotels, constructed directly on the beach, forming a wall which cuts off the westerly breeze."[67]These hotels have proliferated in the subsequent decades, especially along the aptly-named Sheraton Beach and north to Hilton Beach. The Ayalon Expressway is lined with skyscrapers, as is the area where Rothschild Boulevard ends at Herzl Street. In the Manshiya area, two hotels, the Dan Panorama (1979) and the David Intercontinental hotel (1999), dominate the mostly open area by Charles Clore Park.

Hotels seen from Charles Clore Park

It was in the 1980s that the historical importance of the "White City" of the "Bauhaus Style" modernist buildings in the central city became clear. In 2003, the UNESCO World Heritage commission recommended labelling Tel Aviv's core of 1930s-1950s High-Modernist buildings a World Heritage site. This UNESCO designation became official in 2004; this prestigious label for Tel Aviv's "White City and its Bauhaus Style percolated all sectors of Israeli public life and slowly became an integral, and then a natural part of Tel Avivian vocabulary."[68]

[67] "T.A. smog said dissipating, but ecology man disagrees," *The Jerusalem Post*, January 12, 1973, page 2.
[68] Sharon Rotbard, *White City, Black City,*11.

Today, Tel Aviv-Yafo is Israel's largest metropolitan area. The Tel Aviv metropolitan area is a seamless stretch of urban development, so it makes sense to think that the city is larger than it actually is: in 2013 the city of Tel Aviv-Yafo had a little under a one-half million residents (414,600) and the metropolitan area had nearly 3.5 million (3,464,100) inhabitants. In the 1967 war, Israel captured all of Jerusalem, and has held it ever since; although Jerusalem is officially Israel's capitol, many nations have sited their embassies in Tel Aviv as a way of recognizing Israel and Palestine's contested claims for Jerusalem (e.g. Eastern Jerusalem, including the Old City area). Tel Aviv is the Middle East's most expensive city to live in, is dependent on automobiles and buses, and alongside areas of enormous wealth are areas of dire poverty—especially in the non-gentrified southern sections. Tel Aviv is experiencing waves of new immigrants and is more ethnically/racially integrated than ever before and the central city has been renovated with public/private money, but overall the city remains a sprawling, automobile-based, city with extremely wealthy areas contrasted with much poverty.

Conclusion

The specific histories of Tulsa and Tel Aviv have many differences, but one overarching similarity: both of them were established not much more than a century ago, and within a decade or two of their founding were promoting themselves as widely known and significant around the world. In a word, both Tulsa and Tel Aviv had city elites and boosters who were able to successfully promote an image of their city's world-wide importance that preceded the actual attainment of that level of importance.

Moreover, Tulsa and Tel Aviv were frontier cities, in that they were established by Europeans and Americans--who saw themselves as civilized—in areas already occupied by Native Americans and Palestinian Arabs. In order to erase memories of the natives' claim to the land of the new cities, Tulsa's and Tel Aviv's founders emphasized the ideal of progress: how their new cities were the physical embodiment of a grand march of civilization and human progress to take over from savagery. These ideals were Manifest Destiny and Zionism. The establishment of Tulsa and Tel Aviv was the result of Euro-American encroachment on land already in use, if not permanently settled; Manifest Destiny and Zionism were the means of justifying that takeover.

Chapter Three

Ideologies

Zionism and Manifest Destiny

Slogans and myths are powerful tools: especially when governments or organizations decide to allocate their resources to re-constructing a society, or a city, to fit that ideal. Much has been made of the "genocide" of Native Americans at the hands of Europeans and Americans and of Palestinian Arabs at the hands of the Israelis, but that vague and strongly negative wording does little to capture the extent and intent of the process by which European-descended Americans settled North America and the Zionists settled Palestine. The heart of the conquest was justified by the overtly positive booster promotion of slogans, myths, and ideologies, which gave a larger meaning to the economic and land-development patterns that gave birth to modern-style cities in the contested "frontier" areas. The cities of Tulsa and Tel Aviv are clear examples of the success of that booster promotion. Manifest Destiny and Zionism—the two primary ideals promoting settlement in North America and Palestine—were at heart nationalist ideologies, or reactions to the intensifying race/ethnicity-based nationalisms that developed in Europe and America in the wake of the American and French Revolutions. To Americans and European-based Jews, Manifest Destiny and Zionism meant nothing less than the material realization of the mythical Promised Land—at the expense, of course of the indigenous peoples.

The Land

The crux of the conflict in both North America and Palestine was right to the land. Both Euro-Jewish and American settlers were dismissive of the claims to the land of the people already living on, or using the land. When the European-based Zionist Jews sought to establish a Jewish State in Palestine, it was in collusion with the British Imperial system so the local Arab peoples were the primary rival. Similarly, Americans in the nineteenth century viewed the indigenous peoples as an obstacle to the spread of their settlements and economic opportunities. By the late-nineteenth century (1880s-1890s), Indian Territory, present-day eastern Oklahoma, was one of the last-remaining frontier areas. For Zionists, the physical land of Palestine had ingrained significance. For Americans, the land of the North American interior was the frontier—the place soon to be civilized by Americans in the name of progress.

In 1893, historian Frederick Jackson Turner publicly declared that the era of the frontier in U.S. history was over. Turner's basis for this argument was that U.S. settlers had taken supremacy over the Native Americans. To Turner, the frontier was "the meeting place between civilization and savagery," and so the closing of the frontier was another way of saying that the United States' Manifest Destiny was essentially achieved. Turner's words bear repeating (from Chapter 1): "The United States lies like a huge page in the history of society. Line by line as we read *from west to east we find the record of social evolution.* It begins with the Indian and the hunter; it goes on to tell of *the disintegration of savagery by the entrance of the trader, the pathfinder of civilization*; we read the annals of the pastoral stage in ranch life; the exploitation of the soil by the raising of unrotated crops of corn and wheat in sparsely settled farming communities; the intensive culture of the denser farm settlement; and finally *the manufacturing organization with city and factory system* [emphasis added]."[69]

Clearly, Turner's interpretation of U.S. settlement adopts a from-above perspective of the analyst looking down dispassionately at recent or contemporary events, in order to describe the wheels of progress turning to reach the European-derived post-Industrial Revolution ideal of civilization. Turner's use of words like savagery sting our contemporary sensibilities, but they were very common in the 1890s; likewise, Turner's conception of the industrial city as the pinnacle of human society seems overly romantic given the problems (obvious even in the 1890s) of industrialized urban areas.

[69] All quotes from Turner's speech are from: http://xroads.virginia.edu/%7EHYPER/TURNER/

When Turner pronounced the end of the frontier in American history in 1893, Indian Territory was one of the very few places in the continental U.S. not yet assimilated; in fact, the land runs in central and western Oklahoma were recent events (1889) or ongoing. Oklahoma was not yet a state in 1893, and the few cities that Turner would have recognized as such are difficult to discern: most of the important cities in Oklahoma circa statehood in 1907 were fledgling settlements in 1893, Tulsa included.

Relevant to Tulsa, Turner's assessment of the U.S frontier in 1893 bears further exploration. Let's begin with Turner's own words.

> Since the days when the fleet of Columbus sailed into the waters of the New World, America has been another name for opportunity, and the people of the United States have taken their tone from the incessant expansion which has not only been open but has even been forced upon them. He would be a rash prophet who should assert that the expansive character of American life has now entirely ceased. Movement has been its dominant fact, and, unless this training has no effect upon a people, the American energy will continually demand a wider field for its exercise. But never again will such gifts of free land offer themselves. For a moment, at the frontier, the bonds of custom are broken and unrestraint is triumphant. There is not *tabula rasa*. The stubborn American environment is there with its imperious summons to accept its conditions; the inherited ways of doing things are also there; and yet, in spite of environment, and in spite of custom, each frontier did indeed furnish a new field of opportunity, a gate of escape from the bondage of the past; and freshness, and confidence, and scorn of older society, impatience of its restraints and its ideas, and indifference to its lessons, have accompanied the frontier. What the Mediterranean Sea was to the Greeks, breaking the bond of custom, offering new experiences, calling out new institutions and activities, that, and more, the ever retreating frontier has been to the United States directly, and to the nations of Europe more remotely. And now, four centuries from the discovery of America, at the end of a

> hundred years of life under the Constitution, the frontier has gone, and with its going has closed the first period of American history.

About the rapidity of the spread of European and American influence in the Americas he said:

> Why was it that the Indian trader passed so rapidly across the continent? ...The trade was coeval with American discovery. The Norsemen, Vespuccius, Verrazani, Hudson, John Smith, all trafficked for furs. The Plymouth pilgrims settled in Indian cornfields, and their first return cargo was of beaver and lumber. ...All along the coast from Maine to Georgia the Indian trade opened up the river courses. Steadily the trader passed westward, utilizing the older lines of French trade. The Ohio, the Great Lakes, the Mississippi, the Missouri, and the Platte, the lines of western advance, were ascended by traders. They found the passes in the Rocky Mountains and guided Lewis and Clark, Fremont, and Bidwell.

Turner was not blind to the impact of the traders on the indigenous peoples, but he largely blamed the decline of the natives on the bloody and ill-conceived actions of the natives themselves. "The trading post left the unarmed tribes at the mercy of those that had purchased firearms -- a truth which the Iroquois Indians wrote in blood, and so the remote and unvisited tribes gave eager welcome to the trader. 'The savages,' wrote La Salle, 'take better care of us French than of their own children; from us only can they get guns and goods.' This accounts for the trader's power and the rapidity of his advance. Thus the disintegrating forces of civilization entered the wilderness. Every river valley and Indian trail became a fissure in Indian society, and so that society became honeycombed." Turner continues: "Long before the pioneer farmer appeared on the scene, primitive Indian life had passed away. The farmers met Indians armed with guns. The trading frontier, while steadily undermining Indian power by making the tribes ultimately dependent on the whites, yet, through its sale of guns, gave to the Indian increased power of resistance to the farming frontier. French colonization was dominated by its trading frontier; English colonization by its farming frontier. There was an antagonism between the two frontiers as between the two nations."

Ultimately, however, Turner's heroic theme prevails: "And yet, in spite of this opposition of the interests of the trader and the farmer, the Indian trade pioneered the way for civilization. The buffalo trail became the Indian trail, and this became the trader's "trace;" the trails widened into roads, and the roads into turnpikes, and these in turn were transformed into railroads." "The trading posts reached by these trails were on the sites of Indian villages which had been placed in positions suggested by nature; and these trading posts, situated so as to command the water systems of the country, have grown into such cities as Albany, Pittsburgh, Detroit, Chicago, St. Louis, Council Bluffs, and Kansas City." One can presume he would have interpreted Tulsa's rapid growth in the early twentieth century along similar lines.

In Palestine, the main Zionist ideologue, Theodore Herzl, provides the most relevant contemporary counterpart to Turner. Herzl was a prolific writer, and his 1896 book *The Jewish State* was an extremely influential Zionist text. In it, in the section "The Occupation of the Land", Herzl outlined the main tenets of the Zionist settlement plan. Like Turner, Herzl had a clear European-history bias, but to Herzl the emphasis was less on idealizing past civilization and more on emphasizing the "scientific" means of achieving progress today. He wrote: "When nations wandered in historic times, they let chance carry them, draw them, fling them hither and thither, and like swarms of locusts they settled down indifferently anywhere. For in historic times the earth was not known to man. But this modern Jewish migration must proceed in accordance with scientific principles." He continued: "Little is left to chance now. Thus we must investigate and take possession of the new Jewish country by means of every modern expedient. As soon as we have secured the land, we shall send over a ship, having on board the representatives of the Society, of the Company, and of the local groups, who will enter into possession at once. These men will have three tasks to perform: (1) An accurate, scientific investigation of all natural resources of the country; (2) the organization of a strictly centralized administration; (3) the distribution of land. These tasks intersect one another, and will all be carried out in conformity with the now familiar object in view."

> The word 'impossible' has ceased to exist in the vocabulary of technical science. Were a man who lived in the last century to return to the earth, he would find the life of today full of incomprehensible magic. Wherever the moderns appear with our inventions, we transform the desert into a garden. To build a city takes in our time as many years as it formerly required centuries; America offers endless examples of this. Distance has ceased to be an obstacle. The spirit of our age has gathered fabulous treasures into its storehouse. Every day this wealth increases. A hundred thousand heads are occupied with speculations and research at every point of the globe, and that any one discovers belongs the next moment to the whole world. We ourselves will use and carry on every new attempt in our Jewish land; and just as we shall introduce the seven-hour day as an experiment for the good of humanity, so we shall proceed in everything else in the same humane spirit, making of the new land a land of experiments and a model State.[70]

Herzl clearly saw the Zionist movement as a state-of-the-art settlement of an already civilized (European-style) people relocating to a new land, or frontier.

The point I wish to make by reproducing Herzl's and Turner's quotes here is this: these men uncritically accepted the ideals of Zionism and Manifest Destiny and endeavored to shape the facts to fit their thesis; in doing so, they created circular arguments in which the future ideal civilization justifies everything required to achieve that plan. The tone of their words is positive and delivered with care to seem scholarly, academic, or objective; this is very similar to (uncritical) European views of the Middle East, or the "Orient." As argued by the Palestinian scholar Edward Said, Europeans commonly perpetuated uncritical negative stereotypes of non-Europeans under the guise of objective knowledge as a means of justifying imperialist or patronizing policies; Said's book *Orientalism* (1978) was a founding book of post-colonial theory. Said, a Palestinian-Arab born in Jerusalem, was also deeply concerned with the Arab-Israeli conflict, and among his

---

[70] All quotes from Herzl's book are from: https://www.jewishvirtuallibrary.org/jsource/Zionism/herzl2.html.

writings are books like *The Question of Palestine* (1979, revised 1992) that denounce Zionism and anti-Palestinian bias in the West.

While Said's writings focus on Palestine, and also the European powers and the United States' influence there, I believe that his larger arguments apply fairly well to North America--it does not take much imagination to see a connection between the views of U.S. Manifest Destiny proponents like Turner and the Zionist proponents that Said criticizes (such as Herzl). This chapter will take the possibility of such a connection seriously and attempt to point out strengths or weaknesses as the case may be.

Palestine

The beginnings of Zionism may be traced to the mixing of Enlightenment-Europe nationalistic fervor with the Jewish peoples' recognition that they were not at home in Europe.

Jewish nationalism was shaped by centuries of abuse, neglect, and persecution in Christian Europe. At times, Jews were accepted and tolerated in nations like France or Germany, but at other times made scapegoats for the nation's problems, rounded up, and killed. The Spanish Inquisition and the Holocaust were merely two particularly large-scale examples. Another example was the York (England) Massacre of 1189-90, in which a whole community of Jews was forced to commit suicide and kill their sons and daughters to avoid an even worse fate. This event was recorded by Ephraim of Bonn:

> Afterwards, in the year 4551 (l. - 4550 = 1190) the Wanders came upon the people of the Lord [i.e. the Jews] in the city of Evoric (York) in England, on the Great Sabbath [before Passover] and the season of the miracle was changed to disaster and punishment. All fled to the house of prayer. Here Rabbi Yom-Tob stood and slaughtered sixty souls, and others also slaughtered. Some there were who commanded that they should slaughter their only sons, whose foot could not tread upon the ground from their delicacy and tender breeding. Some, moreover, were burned for the

> Unity of their Creator. The number of those slain and burned was one hundred and fifty souls, men and women, all holy bodies. Their houses moreover they destroyed, and they despoiled their gold and silver and the splendid books which they had written in great number, precious as gold and as much fine gold, there being none like them for their beauty and splendour. These they brought to Cologne and to other places, where they sold them the Jews.[71]

In the twelfth century, the great Jewish thinker Maimonides (1135-1204) defined the essential characteristics of being a Jew. Maimonides (known as Rambam) was born in Spain, which was then under Muslim control, but later fled to Morocco, Palestine, and Egypt; he was the greatest legal and philosophical thinker of the time. Maimonides studied the *Torah* and distilled Jewish law and the essential characteristics of being Jewish as: thirteen principles of faith, "the fundamental truths of our religion and its very foundations."[72] In exile, Maimonides gave a voice and a direction to the Jews, and offered a definition of their moral and judicial cause and identity. Jews may be forced to live in nations controlled by non-Jews, but there is strength in staying true to one's traditions and identity. Maimonides's legal treatises, based on the *Torah* (and not much on the *Talmud*), formed the basis of Jewish law for several centuries, and heavily influenced the *Shulkhan Arukh* (complied in the sixteenth century by Joseph Caro), which remains the standard legal code of Judaism. The *Shulkhan Arukh* was the first to list and define Jewish law according to the varied customs of Sephardic (Spain, Portugal) and Ashkenazic (Germany, France, Poland) Jews.

---

[71] Medieval Sourcebook: Ephraim of Bonn: The York Massacre 1189-90. Text available at: http://sourcebooks.fordham.edu/source/ephr-bonn1.asp.

[72] Here is the list of Maimonides's Thirteen Principles. Belief in the existence of the Creator, be He Blessed, who is perfect in every manner of existence and is the Primary Cause of all that exists. The belief in G-d's absolute and unparalleled unity. The belief in G-d's noncorporeality, nor that He will be affected by any physical occurrences, such as movement, or rest, or dwelling. The belief in G-d's eternity. The imperative to worship Him exclusively and no foreign false gods. The belief that G-d communicates with man through prophecy. The belief that the prophecy of Moses our teacher has priority. The belief in the divine origin of the Torah. The belief in the immutability of the Torah. The belief in divine omniscience and providence. The belief in divine reward and retribution. The belief in the arrival of the Messiah and the messianic era. The belief in the resurrection of the dead. Medieval Sourcebook: Maimonides: The 13 Principles and the Resurrection of the Dead. Text available at: http://sourcebooks.fordham.edu/source/rambam13.asp.

During the Medieval and Early Modern periods in Europe, Jews were socially and politically marginalized. Jews were often forced to live in Jewish-only areas, or *ghettos*, of cities; the first ghetto formed in Northern Italy in the sixteenth century. Moreover, Jews were treated under the law as resident foreigners without political say and their occupations were limited to artisans, traders, or moneylenders. This last example, moneylender, was especially significant because of the Medieval Catholic/Christian belief that lending money at interest was usury, a sin; Christians allowed Jews to be moneylenders, which was necessary for the economy, but with the vicious cycle of seeing Jews as sinful because they performed that (dirty) economic role. With the increased economic status of Jews, persecution increased. In 1204 the papacy required Jews to wear distinctive clothing—a common theme with later Nazi Anti-Semitic laws. By the fourteenth century, Christians in England, France, and Spain began to expel Jewish communities. Many Jews relocated to Eastern Europe (Greater Lithuania, including today's Poland and eastern Russia) and to the Ottoman Empire, where they were able (at least at first) to put their commercial and economic skills to use.

Palestine, 1776

The Industrial Revolution (c. 1760) and the rise of industrial capitalism improved Jewish status in Western Europe somewhat; Jews took part in the new economic systems. Also, the Enlightenment and the rising secularization of society lessened the religious-based persecution of Jews. Moreover, the nationalist ideals of Enlightenment-influenced political ideology enabled Jews to assimilate within nations; for example, in France because the French Revolution swept away many Old Regime prejudices.

By the nineteenth century, the situation of Jews had noticeably improved in most Western European countries. You could say that the rise of Anti-Semitism in France and Germany in the second-half of the nineteenth century was especially difficult for Jews to understand because many of them had assimilated so successfully.

The situation of Jews in Eastern Europe—in particular Russia and Poland—was noticeably worse by about 1850. There was a mass exodus (or forced deportation) of Jews from Russia and Poland in the late-nineteenth century, to the United States, to Western Europe, and increasingly (although in comparatively small numbers) to Palestine.

Some Jews had lived in Palestine for centuries under the rule of the Ottoman Empire. The *Tanzimat* reform of the early nineteenth century had improved their situation somewhat, but in general they were a small minority without substantial rights under Ottoman law. The increased immigration of Jews from Europe (in particular from Russia and Poland) alarmed the Ottomans and the native Arabs; therefore, strict legal restrictions were enforced (although not always effectively) on Jewish immigration in the late-nineteenth century.

Many historians have echoed the Zionist view of Palestine under Ottoman rule as a backwater area or frontier area of minor importance, besides the holy sites in Jerusalem. Pre 1919, the Ottoman administration of Palestine was divided into several divisions or *Sanjaks;* the Independent Sanjak of Jerusalem controlled the southern area including the seaports of Jaffa and Gaza and the all-important Holy City of Jerusalem. Tel Aviv, which was founded a few miles north of Jaffa, would have been on the border of the Sanjak of Nablus, which was part of a larger administration unit: the Vilayet of Beirut. In general, the Ottoman rulers saw the area of Palestine as unimportant due to the lack of revenue to be raised there, the area's minor strategic importance, and its imprecise borders. The main caveat to this view is that the city of Jerusalem was an international magnet for religious pilgrims--Muslim, Christian, and Jewish—and Jaffa was a primary seaport for visitors to Jerusalem; the area was very important for that reason.

After 1841, the Ottomans tightened their rule of the area, increased the status of the Sanjak of Jerusalem, and allowed the European powers—Russia, Prussia/Germany, England, France—to increase economic investments in Palestine. As a result, the economy grew in the latter-half of the nineteenth century, and the "modernization" process of the region began under Ottoman rule. Under Sultan Abdul Hamid II (1876-1909), many changes occurred, especially improvements of the communications infrastructure (e.g. telegraphs), education, in the economy (e.g. international/export trade) and transportation infrastructure (e.g. roads, ports, bridges). Most significantly, the Ottomans allowed European companies to build infrastructure projects in Palestine: for example, the railroad built between Jaffa and Jerusalem in 1892. In short, the modernization process of Palestine began before the arrival of the Zionists.

Zionism was a secular movement, based on Jewish ethnicity and not on religion. The movement began as a reaction to increasing Anti-Semitism in Europe, and it was a thoroughly westernized project. To the Zionists, nuances of Ottoman law were unimportant or backward—they modeled themselves off European standards.

The Ottomans had a complex system of laws, which prevented non-native Jews from immigrating to Palestine and purchasing land; when Zionist Jews began ignoring or transgressing these laws, local Arabs grew frustrated and saw the Jews increasingly as a threat.

Despite Ottoman laws, Jewish immigrants from Europe were often able to buy unpalatable land: such as marshes to drain. The Zionists who settled in rural areas typically established small communes, or Kibbutz, based on the ideal of hard work and devotion to working the land. According to Zionist leader Chaim Weizmann—who served as Israel's first President from 1949-1952—"It seems as if God has covered the soil of Palestine with rocks and marshes and sand, so that its beauty can only be brought out by those who love it and will devote their lives to healing its wounds."[73] At first glance this sentiment is laudable: Weizmann (writing in 1941 about his first visit to Palestine in 1907) demonstrates a clear attachment to the land, as you would expect of an

[73] Chaim Weizmann, *Trial and Error: The Autobiography of Chaim Weizmann* (New York: Harper and Row, 1959), 371.

articulate Zionist. Edward Said, however, in *The Question of Palestine* debunks such a simple interpretation; Said sees Weizmann's "thesis about the land of Palestine" as betraying its author's biases.

> The context of this [Weizmann's] remark, however, is a sale made to the Zionists by a wealthy absentee landlord (the Lebanese-Sursuk family) of unpromising marshland. Weizman admits that this particular sale was of *some*, by no means a great deal, of Palestine, yet the impression he gives is of a *whole* territory essentially unused, unappreciated, misunderstood (if one can use such a word in this connection). Despite the people who lived on it, Palestine was therefore *to be made* useful, appreciated, and understandable. The native inhabitants were believed [by the Zionists] curiously to be out of touch with history and, it seemed to follow, they were not really present.[74]

Said goes on to quote another of Weizmann's remarks about Palestine, which also bears repeating: "A dolorous country it was on the whole, one of the most neglected corners of the miserably neglected Turkish Empire. Its total population was something above six hundred thousand of which about eighty thousand were Jews. The latter lived mostly in the cities…But neither the colonies nor the city settlements in any way resembled, as far as vigor, tone and progressive spirit are concerned, the [Zionist] colonies and settlements of our day." Said points out that by "neglect" Weizmann means "to describe Palestine's native inhabitants, [despite] the fact of whose residence there is not a sufficient reason to characterize Palestine as anything but an essentially empty and patient territory, awaiting people who can show a proper care for it."[75]

In 1917, as the First World War was coming to a close, the European Powers began making plans for how to divvy up control of the defeated Ottoman Empire. As part of the Sykes-Picot agreement reached with France (which would assume control of the Northern section, today's Lebanon and Syria), Great Britain would assume control of the Southern section, with Palestine under an Allied Condominium where "there shall be

[74] Edward Said, *The Question of Palestine* (New York: Vintage Books, 1979; reprint 2002). 85.
[75] Ibid. 85.

established an international administration, the form of which is to be decided upon after consultation with Russia, and subsequently in consultation with the other allies, and the representatives of the sheriff of Mecca."[76] The British did meet with Arab leaders, specifically the correspondence between Sir Henry McMahon and Sharif Husain of Arabia, but failed to honor any promises made. In practice, the British assumed control of Palestine as well.

Prior to the ratification of official British control of the area, the British Foreign Secretary, Arthur James Balfour, wrote a letter to Lord Rothschild, a wealthy Zionist sympathizer, on November 2nd, 1917 to declare Great Britain's sympathetic view to the Zionists' project of establishing a Jewish State in in Palestine. This brief statement, known as the Balfour Declaration, virtually ensured a secure foothold for Zionism. The entirety of Lord Balfour's letter follows:

> I have much pleasure in conveying to you, on behalf of His Majesty's Government, the following declaration of sympathy with Jewish Zionist aspirations which has been submitted to, and approved by, the Cabinet.
>
> His Majesty's Government view with favour the establishment in Palestine of a national home for the Jewish people, and will use their best endeavours to facilitate the achievement of this object, it being clearly understood that nothing shall be done which may prejudice the civil and religious rights of existing non-Jewish communities in Palestine, or the rights and political status enjoyed by Jews in any other country.
>
> I should be grateful if you would bring this declaration to the knowledge of the Zionist Federation.[77]

In the wake of Balfour's declaration of British sympathy for a Jewish State in Palestine, the Zionists celebrated and stepped up their efforts to obtain land in Palestine and settle it.

---

[76] The text of the Sykes-Picot Agreement is available at: http://www.mideastweb.org/mesykespicot.htm.
[77] An online reproduction of Lord Balfour's letter is available at: http://www.zionism-israel.com/Balfour_Declaration_1917.htm.

Tel Aviv's founding, and merging with existing Jewish neighborhoods was as part of the Zionist movement's settlement of Palestine with the intention of establishing a Jewish State there. Tel Aviv flourished under the British-Mandate government in the 1920s and 1930s, and during those years it developed ambitious plans to model and compete with European cities: e.g. commissioning Bauhaus or International Style modernist Architecture. Zionism was a direct offshoot of European Imperialism and the European Enlightenment, and during the Mandate period, the Zionists sought to build Tel Aviv on par with the great cities of Europe that they were familiar with in France, Germany, and England. One of the main factors in Tel Aviv's rapid growth into a city with high population density and high land values was land speculation, due in large part to the scramble of European-descended Jews to relocate there.

During the 1920s and 1930s, Tel Aviv's boosters aggressively promoted the city as "The First Hebrew City," and as a destination city that captured attention worldwide. Tel Aviv's first mayor, Meir Dizengoff, was one of these promoters. Zionist boosters like Dizengoff propagated this ideal of Tel Aviv as the "mythic city" at international conferences, with varied effects. On a 1923 visit to the United States, for example, Mayor Dizengoff was greeted by Zionist supporters with the assertion that Tel Aviv was commonly known there as the "First Hebrew City," However, the propaganda emphasizing the city's importance did not reach everyone; for example, in an amusing example, after hearing the brash self-promotion of Tel Aviv's boosters, in a satirical statement the Astronomical Observatory at Greenwich's noted that no one at the Observatory knew where Tel Aviv was.[78] The disparity was real between Zionist propaganda of Tel Aviv and the reality of the city's relative unimportance worldwide to anyone except for Zionists. In the 1930s and 1940s, however, Tel Aviv morphed from a Zionist neighborhood/suburb of Jaffa into a metropolis. By 1950, Tel Aviv had literally conquered and swallowed up Jaffa.

After 1948, immigration into Israel skyrocketed because Israel opened its borders to all Jews. This meant a lack of infrastructure nation-wide to accommodate all the immigrants. In response, policymakers pushed the adoption of rural-development policies

[78] Maoz Azaryahu, "Tel Aviv: Mythography of a City," 36.

(the Sharon Plan), as well as infrastructure updates to urban areas, and implementing existing development laws such as the Public Health Ordinance Law of 1940. It is within this context of rapid change—yet continuing commitment to European-influenced ideas of development—that Tel Aviv's urban-development policies should be understood.

After merging with Jaffa in 1950, Tel Aviv developed a multi-faced urban character that belied its claim to being the First Hebrew City. Unified Tel Aviv-Yafo presented a more complex face to the city's identity, as the history of the old city of Jaffa stretched back thousands of years, connecting with the ancient Jewish and the largely-ignored Arab past(s), while Tel Aviv's contemporary architecture was modernist and oriented toward the future. Part of the new urban atmosphere of Tel Aviv was a vibrant nightlife, and a commercial network ranging from coffee shops to beach-front resorts. These features did not fit city boosters' Zionist image, and were absent from promotion materials advertising Tel Aviv's image. A central part of Tel Aviv's continuing representation as the First Hebrew City and symbol of Zionism was ignoring the wrinkles that did not conform to the official image.

North America

Historians today generally agree that the Native Americans migrated from Asia some 30,000 to 40,000 years ago, and were initially hunter-gathering or foraging peoples. These peoples slowly spread out over the American continents and diversified. Various tribes, or culturally distinct groups, developed independently--although often in contact with other tribes--to fit with location-specific geography, climate, and natural resources. In many locales, the nomadic hunter-gatherer lifestyle gradually gave way to agricultural settlements and cities. Yet, Europeans were not apt to describe the natives as anything but hunter-foragers. In the "myth of western conquest, all Indians were nomadic," although "peoples with other strategies for procuring a living" vastly outnumbered peoples that were strictly foragers and hunter-gatherers.[79]

Nevertheless, some cities in the Americas, such as Cahokia near today's East St. Louis near the banks of the Mississippi River, were large by European standards of the time, although Europeans were largely silent on that fact. The first European explorers came into direct contact with two of the greatest civilizations of the Americas: the Aztec and the Inca. The conquest of the Aztec especially demonstrates the European (in this case, Spanish) blatant disregard of non-familiar cultures and societies; to the Spanish, the flourishing city of Tenochtitlan was simply a place with gold and valuables to plunder and where the people were ripe for conversion and enslavement.

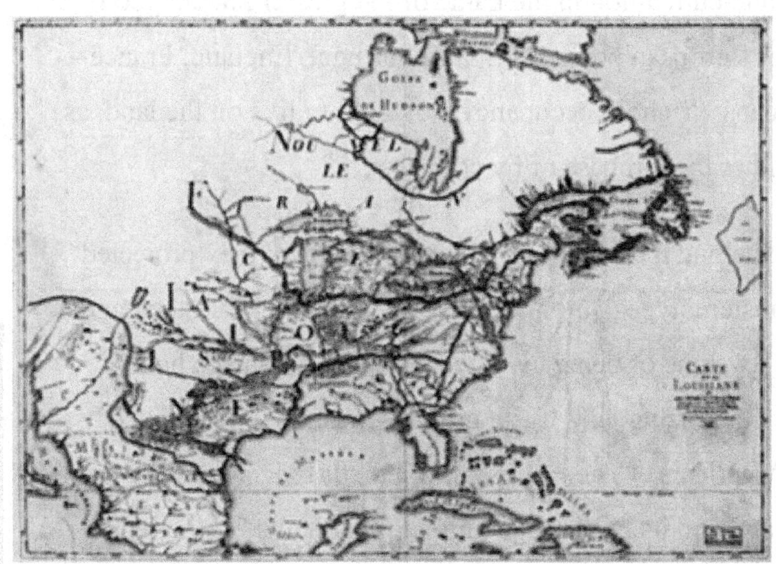

French exploration in North America

European nations began exploring and exploiting Native American lands soon after the discovery of the Americas by Christopher Columbus (1492). Spain, France, and England all claimed vast holdings in the land area now part of the United States of America. The present-day site of Tulsa was part of the area initially claimed by the Spanish, then transferred to French control and became part of a vast and lucrative fur-trading network. This area was eventually purchased by the United States in 1803 under the direction of President Thomas Jefferson. The Louisiana Purchase, as Jefferson's purchase of the land was called, opened up the U.S.'s claim to the interior and western shore of the North American continent. At the southern border of the purchase

[79]Robert V. Hine and John Mack Faragher, *Frontiers: A Short History of the American West* (New Haven: Yale University Press, 2007), 2.

was the area of today's Oklahoma, just north of the Red River. The Mississippi River marked the eastern border, and so the purchase allowed the United States to control the continent's interior, as the rivers branching off from the Mississippi offered access into the "unsettled" frontier lands. The Arkansas River, which flows into the Mississippi River after making its way from the Rocky Mountains of Colorado, was one of these important rivers—and it was on its banks that Tulsa was founded.

One of the most important differences was that Native Americans did not have a conception of private ownership of land such as Europeans did; Europeans exploited this fact over and over in the following decades. To Europeans, and to Americans, the largely uncultivated land area on which indigenous tribes lived was still wilderness: land, therefore, open to settlement and cultivation in the name of the greater human good, or civilization. Yet, all the major European powers—Spain, Portugal, England, France--recognized the Native Americans' "right to occupancy," or right to live on the land, as "alienable in but two ways, either by purchase or by conquest."[80]

When English colonists settled along the east coast of North America, they projected their own cultural and societal stereotypes onto the natives. Cultivating livestock and agriculture was an important keystone of being civilized for these colonists; having steady farms and town-sites with grazing land was a primary means they separated themselves from the Native Americans. "The English saw a disturbing symmetry between the savagery of the land and its human and animal inhabitants." America, according to colonist Robert Cushman in 1621, "is spacious and void" because the Native Americans "do but run over grass, as do the foxes and wild beasts." Such views "fueled colonists' own claims to the land" and were common among the Puritan colonists of Massachusetts Bay; for example, John Winthrop said the "savage people" have no claim to the land "for they inclose no ground, neither have they cattell to maintayne it, but remove their dwellings as they have occasion." Winthrop used biblical history to argue that a permanent and sedentary use of the land—such as Europeans commonly did by the seventeenth century—was the equivalent to a "civil claim" to the land; in effect,

---

[80] Helen M. Hunt, *A Century of Dishonour: A Sketch of the United States Government's Dealings with some of the North American Tribes* (London: Chatto & Windus, Piccadilly, 1881), 9-11.

Winthrop argued that the European-based settlers knew how to domesticate, or subdue, the land, so they had the superior claim.[81] Yet, for Winthrop and the Puritan settlers he led, their settlement in the New World was a spiritual and religious labor: to build a pure society. The physical land was in itself a worldly concern, a source of potential corruption, and ultimately the means of determining the settlement's success. Failure, Winthrop warned, would mean that "we shall perish out of the land we are crossing the sea to possess" and, specifically, God would punish through "crop failures, epidemics, grass-hoppers, caterpillars, torrid summers, arctic winters, Indian wars, hurricanes, shipwrecks, accidents, and (most grievous of all) unsatisfactory children."[82]

Winthrop's successors—the Brahmin of Massachusetts Bay—like Increase Mather found many examples of such failure, decline, and punishment; curiously, in their "Jeremiads" exhorting adherence to God's plan, they advocated continued practices of "modernization" and adaptation. In the New World, these prominent men realized: "Changes there had to be: adaptations to the environment, expansion of the frontier, mansions constructed, commercial adventures undertaken. These activities" "were thrust upon the society by American experience." "Land speculation meant not only wealth but also dispersion of people, and what was to stop the march of settlement?" Winthrop's covenant doctrine "had been utterly oblivious of what the fact of a frontier would do for imported order, let alone for a European mentality." Thus, the importance of the Jeremiads was that "under the guise of this mounting wail of sinfulness, this incessant and never successful cry for repentance, the Puritans launched themselves upon the process of Americanization."[83]

Between 1680 and 1770, America modernized into a land of sophisticated economic, social, and political, and material complexity; its foundation was European society and culture, but America developed its unique customs and expressions. The upshot is that American society by this period "exhibited the modern penchant for power, control, and authority over both humanity and nature that brooked few limitations" and where

---

[81] Virginia DeJohn Anderson, "King Phillip's Herds" in Stanley N. Katz et al, *Colonial America: Essays in Politics and Social Development 5th edition* (Boston: McGraw Hill, 2001) 334.

[82] Perry Miller, *Errand into the Wilderness* (Cambridge, MA: The Belknap Press of Harvard University Press, 1956; reprinted 1984), 6.

[83] Ibid. 9.

"ethnically and nationally diverse" peoples had developed "transatlantic and international economies that supported a vigorous domestic trade and production."[84]

During this era of transformation, or modernization, Native Americans living in the British mainland settlements and frontiers—throughout the Midwest, the South, and the Appalachian regions--adapted their economies to accommodate the "shift from episodic European presence" to an "overwhelming European presence and insistent westward push"; the changes made Indian and European economies "fatally interdependent." European-descended settlers increasingly wanted land, and found ways to "dispossess …by degrees" the natives of their territory. The fur trade, in particular, "created a series of dependency relationships with the Europeans in America—never complete but increasingly powerful—that shaped far more than economics." By the seventeenth century, "Indians living near Europeans consumed substantial amounts of European goods, from utensils and cloth to firearms and ammunition," although the "far interior regions" of the Midwest were slow to reach this level of interdependence (circa 1700). As Europeans spread west, Native Americans in the highly settled eastern regions had less to trade, and fell victim to selling their lands in order to fund their newfound European tastes; for example, in 1730 leaders of the Mohawks in New York wrote "our hearts grieves us when we Consider what small parcel of Lands is remaining to us."[85]

From 1776 through 1783 the American colonies successfully rebelled against Great Britain and became the United States of America; this upsetting of the power balance foreshadowed problems for Native Americans. The original thirteen states were along the eastern seaboard, and stretched westward to include parts of the Appalachian Mountains, although the Ohio River Valley and Great Lakes were also somewhat settled. Whereas England had largely respected the tribes "right to occupancy" of the land, and the French were interested mostly in trading, the Americans were focused more on settling western lands and establishing claim to all palatable land. Nevertheless, "The United States

---

[84] Jon Butler, *Becoming America: The Revolution Before 1776* (Cambridge, MA: Harvard University Press, 2000), 2.
[85] Ibid. 65-67.

adopted the same principle" and "recognized, accepted, and acted upon this theory" and this was the basis of U.S. treaties with Native American tribes prior to 1871.[86]

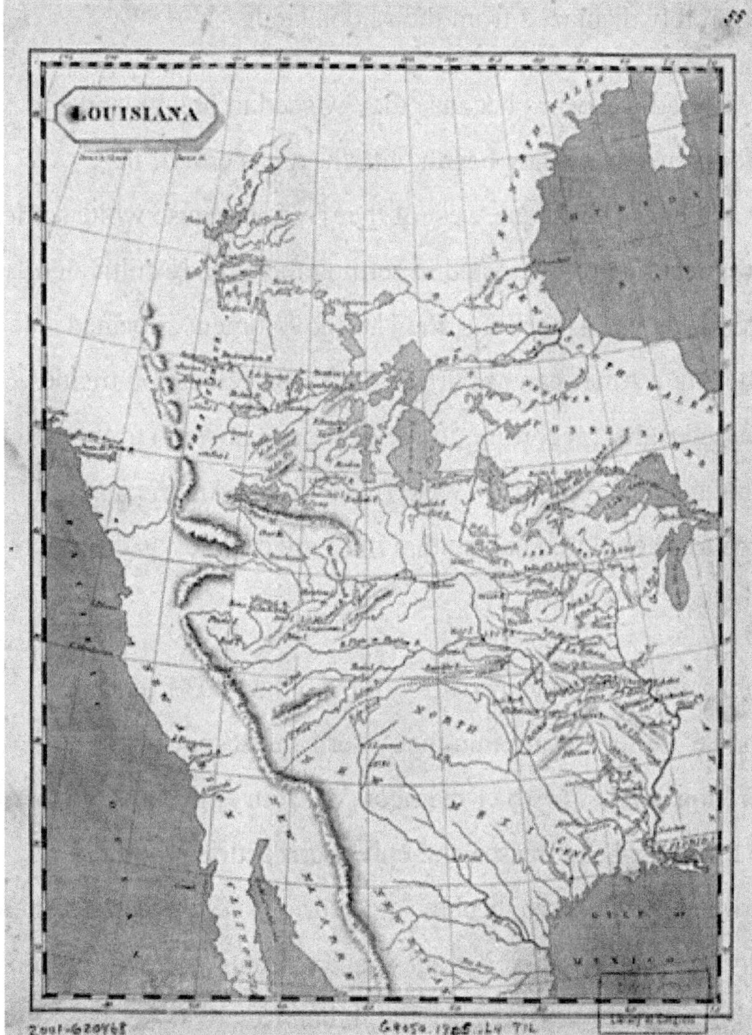

Louisiana Territory, 1805

The U.S. purchase of the Louisiana Territory from France added levels of complexity to this concept of Native Americans' right to possess absolute claim to the land on which they lived and used. The U.S. government had purchased this large area of land legally from France, but how valid had the French claim to that land actually been? France and Spain had both claimed the territory in question, as part of the European colonial system, but in truth they had little lasting presence on the ground except for trading posts and exploration routes. The diverse Native American tribes lived on this land area relatively unencumbered by the French (or, earlier, the Spanish) and hence the Louisiana Purchase was largely a theoretical purchase: a purchase of the right to claim, among the European nations, exclusive right to claim that land area; actually settling the land first required the removal of Native Americans living on it. For nearly one-hundred years, the major use of

[86] Helen M. Hunt, *A Century of Dishonour,* 11, 27.

the land area of Indian Territory, or today's state Oklahoma, was to serve as a relocation place for Native Americans forcibly displaced from their homelands.

European-descended settlers spread westward because they wished to obtain land and thus provide economically for themselves: they began with the areas east of the Mississippi and only afterward began the spread west of the river. Because white settlers in the early-nineteenth century were more interested in settling the already cultivated lands of the Deep South held by Native Americans, the U.S. government allocated today's area of Oklahoma to Native American as part of the forced-relocation treaties. The United States had purchased rights (according to the European powers) to the (later) area of Oklahoma in 1803, but the area remained "wilderness" in the American imagination, or a frontier area to be explored and settled in future decades as the newly independent United States grew.

The Plains Indians native to the area of Indian Territory prior to the 1803 Louisiana Purchase were "nearly unknown" to Europeans and the Americans despite some European trading and exploration parties. In 1821 members of Plains tribes visited Washington D.C., and their feathered headdresses and chivalrous actions captured American imagination: a Pawnee, Petalesharo, became a celebrity.[87] Nevertheless, their stereotype among Americans was that of "noble savages" and as entertainment. Within a decade of the Plains delegation's visit in Washington, the Indian Removal Act was signed giving the Five Civilized Tribes official claim to most of the land in Indian Territory.

Indian Territory was in the south-eastern section of the Louisiana Territory, fairly accessible from the major river-trade networks of the Mississippi River. One of the ironies of Oklahoma history is that despite initial American assumptions of being among the first of the new states fashioned from the Louisiana Territory it was the last. After 1830, Indian Territory was largely reserved for the Five Civilized Tribes and other indigenous peoples and so kept separate from the spread of U.S. settlement for several decades. This area was one of the last continental states (the 46th) to be admitted to the

[87] Wendell H. Oswalt, *This Land Was Theirs: A Study of Native Americans,* Seventh Edition (Boston: McGraw-Hill Mayfield, 2001), 48.

Union: Oklahoma, in 1907. The reasons for Oklahoma's delayed American settlement had more to do with politics than geography.

The United States increased its military and administrative presence in Indian Territory during the 1810s-1820s. Most significant was the 1817 establishment of Fort Smith in Arkansas, located on the banks of the Arkansas River, which became the center of U.S. law and justice for Indian Territory as well as a regional military base; also significant was the 1824 establishment of Fort Gibson at the Three Forks region at the intersection of the Neosho (Grand) River and the Arkansas River, just downstream of where the Verdigris River meets the Arkansas. In 1824 the U.S. government created the Bureau of Indian Affairs (BIA) within the War Department in order to civilize Native Americans; in 1849 the BIA was relocated under civilian control as part of the Department of the Interior.

The settlement of Indian Territory sped up after the Indian Removal Act of 1830. This Act required the well-established tribes, often called the Civilized Tribes (Creek, Cherokee, Seminole, Choctaw, Chickasaw), residing in the states of the U.S. South to give up their lands, farms, and towns and move westward to the area that would become Indian Territory. With the forced relocation, or "The Trail of Tears," the Five Civilized Tribes courageously did their best to recreate their homelands in Indian Territory. Here, "they established farms, ranches and plantations; built towns, churches and schools; linked the five Indian nations together with a well-developed system of trade and communications. Even here in the wilderness they governed themselves with their own laws and their own courts and continued their progress along the road to a civilized society."[88]

When Washington Irving visited the (future) site of Tulsa in 1832 he commented on the eventuality of the United States' spread across that frontier. While exploring the bend of the Arkansas River where Tulsa would be founded (on October 12), Irving related a story about honey: about how the natives saw bee hives as a symbol of (American) land-development patterns and cultivation. Irving probably intended this story as a parable of

---

[88] William Butler, *Tulsa 75: A History of Tulsa* (Tulsa: The Metropolitan Tulsa Chamber of Commerce, 1975), 19.

the sweet side (both as equating the spread of the Americans as progress, and quite literally) of Manifest Destiny. Irving's parable bears quotation at length.

> The beautiful forest in which we were encamped abounded in bee-trees; that is to say, trees in the decayed trunks of which wild bees had established their hives. It is surprising in what countless swarms the bees have over-spread the Far West, within but a moderate numbers of years. The Indians consider them the harbinger of the white man, as the buffalo is of the red man; and say that, in proportion as the bee advances, the Indian and the buffalo retire. We are always accustomed to associate the hum of the bee-hive with the farm-house and flower-garden, and to consider these industrious little animals as connected with the busy haunts of man, and I am told that the wild bee is seldom to be met with at any great distance from the frontier. They have been the heralds of civilization, steadfastly preceding it as it advanced from the Atlantic borders, and some of the ancient settlers of the West pretend to give the very year when the honey-bee first crossed the Mississippi. The Indians with surprise found the mouldering trees of their forests suddenly teeming with ambrosial sweets, and nothing, I am told, can exceed the greedy relish with which they banquet for the first time upon this unbought luxury of the wilderness.
>
> At present [in 1832 at the future site of Tulsa] the honey-bee swarms in myriads, in the noble groves and forests which skirt and intersect the prairies, and extend along the alluvial bottoms of the rivers. It seems to me as if these beautiful regions answer literally to the description of the [Biblical] land of promise, "a land flowing with milk and honey"; for the rich pasturage of the prairies is calculated to sustain herds of cattle as countless as the sands upon the sea-shore, while the flowers with which

they are enameled render them a very paradise for the nectar-seeking bee.[89]

Irving had a travelogue tone to his account, but he attempted to portray the natives with dignity. "In fact, the Indians that I have had the opportunity of seeing in real life are quite different from those described in poetry. They are by no means the stoics that they are represented." "In the course of my journey along the frontier, I have had repeated opportunities of noticing their excitability and boisterous merriment." Therefore, "the Indian of poetical fiction is like the shepherd of pastoral romance, a mere personification of imaginary attributes."[90]

Misunderstandings between the Native Americans and European-descended Americans were common. Americans, such as Washington Irving described, ascribed stereotypical features to Native Americans, and often judged them for not being Europeanized enough or for not understanding American ways. It was illogical for Americans to assume that, because they had bought the Louisiana Purchase from the French that therefore all the natives would agree to that. In his account, Irving described the (future) area of Tulsa as un-settled by white Americans, yet he also described it as "our spacious forests" to make clear America's ownership of the region.[91]

Even in settled communities, most tribes did not have comparable political hierarchies to the European powers: institutions like a standing army, a bureaucracy, or an all-powerful monarch; therefore, Europeans "had great difficulty understanding the authority of a tribal chief," because instead of the accumulation of "wealth and power," the chief's status was judged by "how well he disbursed resources" among clans.[92]

The first recorded permanent settlement at the site of Tulsa was established in 1836 by a band of Creeks who had been forced to relocate to Indian Territory. These Creeks, led by Chief Opothle Yahola, were the Lochapoka. A 1975 history commissioned by the Tulsa Metropolitan Chamber of Commerce described the Lochapokas' founding of Tulsa as

---

89 Washington Irving, *A Tour on the Prairies*, 1835.
90 Ibid.
91 Ibid.
92 Hine and Faragher, *Frontiers,* 3.

follows: "The council fire on the banks of the Arkansas River was consecrated with the ashes of old Tulsey Town [in Alabama], brought to the site by the Creek Medicine Man. Thus the present metropolitan city of Tulsa was born." [93]

It is accurate that the Lochapoka established a village on the eventual site of Tulsa, but it is inaccurate to connect the Lochapoka's council fire with the establishment of the present-day "metropolitan city" of Tulsa. Most of the Lochapoka were pushed out of the area before Tulsa was founded in 1882, as an American outpost settlement. To draw an exact line between Tulsa and the Lochapoka settlement is to promote the booster myth or the outdated thesis of Frederick Jackson Turner that it is the "natural course" of progress and civilization that the Indian settlement paves the way for, but must give way to, the American city. What is clear about the Lochapoka founding story is that it is a favorite of the city's elite families, many of whom are descendants of the early Anglo-American settlers; the Council Oak, as the tree chosen for the ritual fire is named, "marks the spot of Tulsa's birth" and by 1975 "stands in the shadow of a circular-design, 32-story skyscraper" at the corner of 18th and Cheyenne Streets, on the southern edge of Tulsa's downtown district. Perhaps the Council Oak is a favorite symbol of the city's history because it is a tangible reminder of a safe and secure pre-history.

John Louis O'Sullivan, a popular editor and columnist, articulated the long-standing American belief in the God-given mission of the United States to lead the world in the transition to democracy. He called this America's "manifest destiny"; Europeans would term a similar pro-Western expansion policy "modernization." In a 1839 article he wrote:

> The far-reaching, the boundless future will be the era of American greatness. In its magnificent domain of space and time, the nation of many nations is destined to manifest to mankind the excellence of divine principles; to establish on earth the noblest temple ever dedicated to the worship of the Most High -- the Sacred and the True. [...]
>
> Yes, we [the United States of America] are the nation of progress, of individual freedom, of universal enfranchisement. Equality of rights is the

[93] William Butler, *Tulsa 75*, 23.

> cynosure of our union of States, the grand exemplar of the correlative equality of individuals; and while truth sheds its effulgence, we cannot retrograde, without dissolving the one and subverting the other. We must onward to the fulfilment of our mission -- to the entire development of the principle of our organization -- freedom of conscience, freedom of person, freedom of trade and business pursuits, universality of freedom and equality. This is our high destiny, and in nature's eternal, inevitable decree of cause and effect we must accomplish it. All this will be our future history, to establish on earth the moral dignity and salvation of man -- the immutable truth and beneficence of God. For this blessed mission to the nations of the world, which are shut out from the life-giving light of truth, has America been chosen; and her high example shall smite unto death the tyranny of kings, hierarchs, and oligarchs, and carry the glad tidings of peace and good will where myriads now endure an existence scarcely more enviable than that of beasts of the field. Who, then, can doubt that our country is destined to be the great nation of futurity?[94]

"American Progress"

In 1845, O'Sullivan applied his faith in the United States to the annexation of Texas and likely addition of California, areas originally colonized by the Spanish, which had only recently become part of Mexico. Texas declared independence from Mexico in 1836, and joined the United States in 1845. The relevant history of

[94] John O'Sullivan, "The Great Nation of Futurity," *The United States Democratic Review* (Volume 6, Issue 23), 426, 429-430.

Texas and California was that white Americans had settled or squatted in the areas for several decades, and taken advantage of the newly independent Mexican nation's weakness to establish Anglo-American settlement and ultimately governance. On the occasion of Texas joining the United States, O'Sullivan declared: the "independence of Texas was complete and absolute. It was an independence, not only in fact, but of right," and California would follow: "Imbecile and distracted, Mexico never can exert any real governmental authority over such a country." O'Sullivan's wording begs further attention: "Texas is now ours." "She comes within the dear and sacred designation of Our Country," but "other nations have undertaken to intrude themselves" "in a spirit of hostile interference against us, for the avowed object of thwarting our policy and hampering our power, limiting our greatness and checking the fulfillment of our *manifest destiny* to overspread the continent allotted by Providence for the free development of our yearly multiplying millions."[95]

The importance of the railroads in the ideology of Manifest Destiny fit directly with Tulsa and Indian Territory because building a transcontinental system of railroads was the initial reason for Tulsa's growth as an American city. The railroads fulfilled the "purpose of binding and holding together in its iron clasp our fast-settling Pacific region with that of the Mississippi valley–the natural facility of the route" and would solidify the United States' claim to the land, including then-off-limits land in Indian Territory.[96] The ideology of America's Manifest Destiny gave credence and fuel to the idea of the frontier within the Great Plains of the North American interior.

White Americans were able to gain a foothold in Indian Territory after the Civil War: because the Civilized Tribes had been split between support of the Union and the Confederacy, in 1866 the U.S. government "renegotiated" its treaties with them and re-designated large sections of land previously reserved to the tribes as "unassigned land" or "No Man's Land"; these areas, in today's central and western Oklahoma, contributed to the growth of American-backed cattle drives

[95] John O'Sullivan, "Annexation," *The United States Magazine and Democratic Review*, Volume 17 (New York: 1845), 5-6.
[96] Ibid. 9-10.

and the building of railroads into the area; "for years the unassigned lands were occupied by owners of large herds without title or without lease of any kind."[97] In 1871, the U.S. Congress "either ashamed of making treaties only to break them, or grudging the time, money and paper it wasted, passed an act to the effect that no Indian tribe should hereafter be considered as a foreign nation with whom the United States might contract a treaty."[98]

To boosters of America's Manifest Destiny like O'Sullivan, the progress, or benefit to humanity, of the United States taking claim to these lands was clear. America was the democratic future, and the counter to the decadent and aristocratic European past. O'Sullivan wrote: "There is no growth in Spanish America! Whatever progress of population there may be in the British Canadas, is only for their own early severance of their present colonial relation to [Great Britain] the little island three thousand miles across the Atlantic; soon to be followed by Annexation [as part of the U.S.], and destined to swell the still accumulating momentum of our progress." To O'Sullivan, the military might of Imperial Europe—"the bayonets and cannon, not only of France and England, but of Europe entire"—was soon to be cancelled out and overcome by "the simple, solid weight of the two hundred and fifty, or three hundred millions–and American millions–destined to gather beneath the flutter of the stripes and stars" in the following decades.

Some Americans did not look at westward expansion as positive. H.B. Whipple, the Episcopalian Bishop of Minnesota and a well-known advocate for Native Americans, wrote in 1881: "Nations, like individuals, reap exactly what they sow; they who sow robbery reap robbery. The seed-sowing of iniquity replies in a harvest of blood. The American people have accepted as truth the teaching that the Indians were a degraded, brutal race of savages, whom it was the will of God should perish at the approach of civilization." So "they so accept the teaching that manifest destiny will drive the Indians from the earth."[99] Meanwhile, Julius H. Seeyle saw that America's "great trouble has

[97] Clarence B. Douglas, *A History of Tulsa* (Chicago: S.J. Clark Publishing Company, 1921), 17.
[98] Helen M. Hunt, *A Century of Dishonour,* 27.
[99] H.B. Whipple, "Preface," Helen M. Hunt, *A Century of Dishonour: A Sketch of the United States Government's Dealings with some of the North American Tribes* (London: Chatto & Windus, Piccadilly, 1881), v-x.

been that we have sought to exact justice from the Indian while exhibiting no justice to him."[100]

The ideology of Manifest Destiny had largely satisfied its claims by 1882, when the Frisco railroad spur to Tulsa was completed. Railroads and rivers were the common means of transportation into Indian Territory, and so white-American settlement commonly followed (and dictated) these routes. Tulsa was located at the curve of the Arkansas River, where it takes a southward bend toward the more navigable Three Forks area by Fort Gibson. Tulsa was also located relatively close to the navigable Verdigris River, which connected the important regional city of Coffeeville, Kansas with Fort Gibson and the nearby newly established city of Muskogee.

The 1882 Frisco railroad spur connected Tulsa with the cities of the Midwest, and opened up its access to economic markets. Cattle were the most important commodity: after 1882, cattle drives up from Texas were able to stop at Tulsa instead of traveling up to more distant stations like Abilene, Kansas. Although the cattle boom was short lived, and did not last more than a few decades, it provided the initial impetus for Tulsa's rapid growth.

Circa 1882, much of the area around Tulsa was sparsely settled. Creek farmers and ranchers lived in the area, but without a clear town site in the vicinity. Consequently, when the white settlers arrived in 1882, they believed that the area was unsettled. The Hall brothers, J.M. and H.C., were the most significant of these initial settlers: J.M. Hall in particular shaped Tulsa's early development, and in his old age he wrote a history of Tulsa's foundational years. H.C. Hall worked for the Frisco Railroad, and upon arriving at the Tulsa site in 1882 he invited his brother to join him. When J.M. arrived, he found a motley collection of tents with railroad workers and merchants who had set up seemingly overnight. These tents soon gave way to more permanent structures. Another of the important initial settlers was Jeff Archer, part white and part Indian, who established a

[100] Julius H. Seeyle, "Introduction," Helen M. Hunt, *A Century of Dishonour: A Sketch of the United States Government's Dealings with some of the North American Tribes* (London: Chatto & Windus, Piccadilly, 1881), 1-5.

general store in Tulsa. Archer, like many of Tulsa's early merchants, took advantage of the opportunity presented by the construction of the railroad spur to make his fortune.

The reason the American settlers moved into Indian Territory in general and to Tulsa in particular after 1882 was make money. Railroad workers temporarily moved there in 1882, and some like J.M. Hall stayed; merchants set up shop there because of the ready market of railroad workers and the cattle trade. Cowboys were seasonal residents of Tulsa; they stayed there at the completion of their cattle drives and spent their earnings on entertainment, drinking, and on material goods available in Tulsa's stores. Before the discovery of oil in 1905 at the Glenn Pool, Tulsa was primarily a merchant-focused town where transient cowboys, workers, and area farmers or ranchers came to spend money. The aforementioned Frisco line crossed the Arkansas River in 1884 and extended to towns westward including Sapulpa, but Tulsa remained the central focus of the area's burgeoning commerce.

With a flourishing economy came permanent settlement: churches, schools, a post office, and a courthouse, as well as comfortable houses. Many of these settlers were of native heritage: for example, the Perryman family, descendants of Chief Benjamin Perryman. Despite the mixed heritage of many settlers, the city of Tulsa developed nearly exclusively in an American, European-based fashion. J.M. Hall described Tulsa in his book *The Beginning of Tulsa* (1927, revised 1933) as settled on a *tabula rasa*: he asserted that no settlement existed in the area before 1882; Hall cited testimony from local Indian men that only one Creek man, Reuben Partridge, had a house at the site of Tulsa, but besides that "no house could be seen here until about August 1, 1882."[101] J.M. Hall arrived in Tulsa in 1882, so had no firsthand knowledge of the area prior to his arrival; for Hall, Tulsa was totally an American town, where Native Americans had been in the general area but had not preempted American settlement of the specific site of Tulsa.

To white American settlers like J.M. Hall, the only settlement that mattered was of the type they were used to and understood: the European-derived modern; therefore, they saw the land as unused and unsettled according to their narrow definition. The Creeks, of

[101] J.M. Hall, *The Beginning of Tulsa,* 6.

course, had clear-cut policies for distributing and allocating land, and in actual practice their land-use circa 1860 was comparable to that of American settlers. Nevertheless, American settlers emphasized the myths that fit their pro-settlement worldview.

According to the typical myth of Oklahoma's American settlement—especially in the central and western parts of the state--the land was an empty void before the American settlers arrived. It was much easier to ignore the "temporary" settlements of the Plains Tribes than it was to ignore the presence of the Civilized Tribes in the eastern sections. The white settlers in Indian Territory circa 1880 "marveled at the beauty and the empty, undisturbed quality of this land they coveted"; "The white settler believed firmly in dominating the land."[102] The upshot of these beliefs was that in the name of short-term economic profit, the white settlers in Indian Territory (and later Oklahoma) "did untold harm to the natural order" and the Dust Bowl of the 1930s may be traced directly to large-scale and ill-conceived clearing, plowing, and ecological-destruction of the land due to the arrival of white settlers in the 1880s.[103]

As white Americans settled in Tulsa, and in Indian Territory in general, many Indian tribes were outraged and felt betrayed by the U.S. government. The Dawes Act (1887) made Native Americans legally American citizens but forced tribes to split up their block allocations of land, and divide the land according to specific tracts among eligible members; the remainder of the land was opened to American settlers through land runs (through the 1889 Indian Appropriation Act) or was available for purchase to anyone. The U.S. government systematically reneged on its treaties with Native American tribes and failed to honor its agreements to allow tribes access to lands in Indian Territory promised *in perpetua* under the Indian Removal Act. The move toward statehood, realized in 1907, further disappointed Native American tribes because the joining of Oklahoma Territory with Indian Territory lessened the power of tribal leaders in the new state government. Furthermore, the combining of Oklahoma and Indian Territory lessened the political significance of existing cities, most which were located in the eastern part of the new state; Muskogee, the capitol of the Indian Agency and site of the

---

[102] H. Wayne Morgan and Anne Hodges Morgan, *Oklahoma: A History* (New York: Norton and Company, 1984), 11.
[103] Ibid. 11-12.

initial U.S. Federal Courthouse, was overlooked in favor of the centrally located town of Guthrie (1907-1910) and the brand-new planned capitol: Oklahoma City (1910-present). Tulsa did not figure significantly in the discussions of siting the new state capitol because it was still a small frontier town at this time.

Relevant to Indian Territory and Tulsa, the process of American settlement proceeded extremely rapidly, and along the lines of the ideal arc described in popular culture. The defining feature of Tulsa was the rapidity of the urban development and desire for wealth (oil, trade) and the high-culture society that the city's early elite associated with wealth.

The discovery of oil in 1905 at the nearby Glenn Pool began Tulsa's meteoric growth spurt. Whereas "most oil towns vanished quickly" because their oil pools dried up, Tulsa "with no oil of her own, became the most permanent of the boomtowns." Instead of relying on a specific oil pool, Tulsa became the primary administration center for the oil industry in the region. Tulsa's boosters "did everything to change Tulsa from a tough cow town in Indian Territory to the petroleum headquarters of the world. In true boomer style, they set their sights on the great cities of the world as future peers and planned accordingly."[104]

In the 1910s-1920s, Tulsa was a quickly growing city in need of infrastructure improvements; these improvements included legal infrastructure such as a courthouse, drinking water aqueducts, and streets laid out on a grid system. The money from oil and related industries quickly transformed the small town into a veritable city, with a downtown full of skyscrapers. Within Tulsa, an elite class consisting of oilmen and their families arose; this new elite sought to transform Tulsa according to their image.

Economic opportunity brought newcomers, and the increased migration of Americans, both white and black, to Tulsa led to problems of disorder and violence. By the 1920s, racial tensions were high in Tulsa—the city had grown in a racially segregated manner. In 1921 a devastating race riot or racial massacre occurred, in the African-American areas north of downtown. Whites were especially at fault for much of the violence—and whole sections of north Tulsa lay in ruins for months afterward. In Tulsa, the main racial/ethnic

[104] Ibid. 159.

tensions were between whites and blacks; Native Americans were left on the margins. Tulsa's rapid growth, however, remained unchecked and its petroleum-centered economy still flourished.

Conclusion

Zionism and Manifest Destiny were of a particular sort of European-derived nationalism, by which Americans and Zionists defined themselves as progressive and civilized and Arabs or Native Americans as non-civilized and so without legitimate claims to the land.

Nationalism is a broad, complex topic, but similarities are evident in what historians deem modern nationalisms since the eighteenth century. All of these nationalisms had: 1) an "imagined community" of common characteristics to unify or bring into being; 2) identification with common traditions, but not necessarily a historical/factual reason of such identification; 3) common language, and sometimes also common ethnic identification; 4) limits to who was included and who was excluded. Most importantly, nationalist ideology required an "other" from which to base the boundaries that constituted who was in and who was out of the limits of the nationalist community: there was always someone excluded.

Imperialism was a clearly negative side to European and American nationalism, as it enabled powerful nations to act on clear-cut categories of inclusion and exclusion based on dualistic views of the world: East/West, traditional/modern, pre-modern/progress, white/non-white, and so on. These convenient fictions, or stereotypes, were essential to the modern European-centered view of nationalism. This sort of dualistic stereotype was a useful tool in justifying Imperial policies such as the blatant exploitation of labor and natural resources in non-European areas. Europeans and Americans justified such exploitation as essentially good under the myth of the civilizing mission and the belief that new technologies meant civilization, modernization and progress.

The rise of Zionism, in particular, rose out of the Jews perceiving that they were the group excluded: in Russia, Poland, Germany, and France, for example, there was strong evidence in support of their view. Zionism, therefore, was Jewish nationalism, but divorced from the land areas in which they lived; Palestine was their ancient homeland (from *Torah* stories and before the 70 AD Roman sack of Jerusalem), but it was also a convenient land area not already claimed by a powerful European nation. The Zionists had complete faith in Europe's scientific methods, and so they saw the native peoples of Palestine as largely irrelevant. Therefore, Zionism was an outgrowth of European Imperialism.

It also makes sense to analyze the United States' westward spread across North America as imperialism—even if the land in question then is now the heartland of America. To put this idea in context, it may be helpful to remember that France saw Algeria as not a colony but to be France itself; however, that belief did not mean that the native Algerians accepted that belief and therefore accepted French rule.

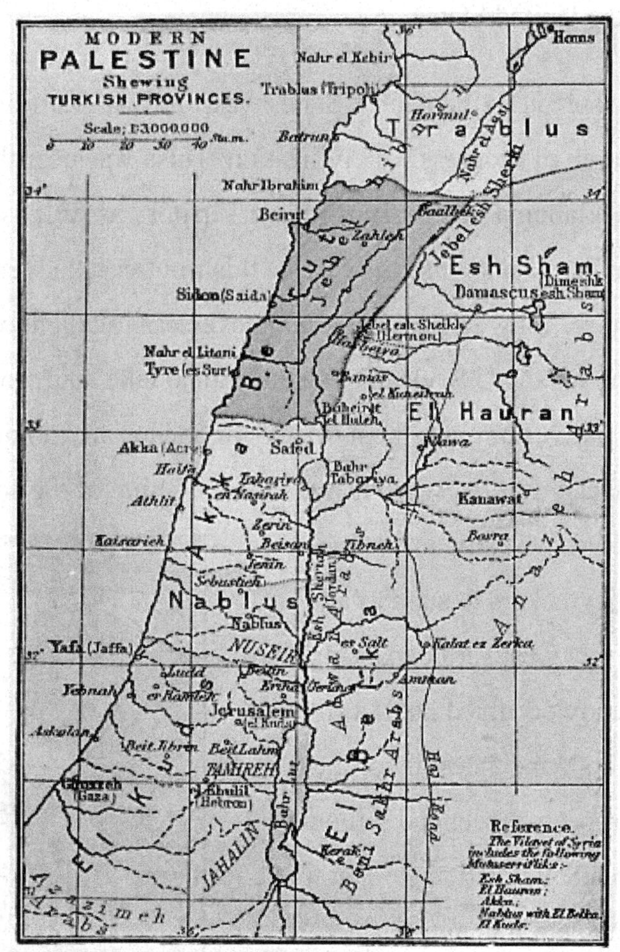

Turkish Palestine, 1887

Typically, foreign-policy scholars of the United States link the beginning of U.S. international involvement with the Spanish-American War, but it is no coincidence that this outward-focused policy corresponded with the time of the supposed closure of the frontier in the 1890s. The 1890s also mark the time when U.S. politicians like Theodore Roosevelt and Albert Beveridge advocated an increased U.S. foreign presence abroad, within the sphere of influence of European powers. Foreign policy historians thus focus on the Spanish American War and the value of war as a tool for spreading both U.S. power and prestige—for example, defeating Spain and assuming administrative control of Spain's former imperial holdings, thereby spreading civilization by extending U.S. administrative control to the peoples of Latin America or the Philippines—but typically have not given similar attention to the United States' takeover of the interior of North America. They would say that through much of the nineteenth century, Americans were focused on westward expansion and the frontier, so the U.S. was largely content to not become involved in "international" conflicts and issues. This is an oversight, due to an emphasis on U.S. foreign policy as the study of areas outside the present-day borders of the United States.

The spread of the United States westward was part of Manifest Destiny, or the so-called "march of progress" of civilization; Tulsa was near the end of that process. In the context of Oklahoma (the heart of Indian Territory as well as the legacy of white settlers and land runs) it makes sense to describe this frontier takeover as imperialism, and the quest for empire. Why do we have to look overseas to talk about "empire" when here in North America the U.S. clearly fought wars to take land from the natives and either "civilize" the natives or erase them. Many Americans are too quick to accept 'Manifest Destiny' as in fact a destiny, when it was in fact nothing of the sort; instead, it was a clear choice by everyday Americans and policymakers to support and portray westward expansion (into already occupied land) as normal, natural, and a destiny of the European-descended settlers to spread civilization.[105] But to the American Indian tribes, the United States was the aggressor.

Indian Territory cigarette card, c. 1888

[105] William O. Walker, *National Security and Core Values in American History,* 33-38.

A major reason this imperialism is difficult for Americans to admit is because after 1871 the United States' official stance is that Native American tribes do not qualify as a "foreign nation" with whom the United States might contract a treaty. This 1871 decision was all the more remarkable due to Congress' long history of making and breaking treaties with various tribes; Helen Hunt Jackson, a well-known authority on the plight of Native American tribes, wrote in her critical 1881 book *A Century of Dishonor* that Congress passed that law in 1871 because they must have been "ashamed of making treaties only to break them" and were "grudging the time, money and paper it wasted" on sham treaties with tribes. After 1871, the United States government referred to "agreements" and "conventions" with Native American tribes instead of making "treaties," but "the difference is only in name." These signed documents "stated, in a succession of numbered articles, promises of payment of moneys, and surrenders and cessions of land by both parties; were to be ratified by Congress before taking effect; and were understood by the Indians agreeing to them to be as binding as if they had been called treaties.[106]

In light of the United States' failure to deal justly with Native American tribes, Hunt's primary argument in *A Century of Dishonor* was that to Indian tribes "the repeated broken faith of the United States Government toward them" was imperialistic in that the U.S. virtually stole tribal land by force and without proper compensation.

> The history of the United States Government's repeated violations of faith with the Indians thus convicts us, as a nation, not only of having outraged the principles of justice, which are the basis of international law; and of having laid ourselves open to the accusation of both cruelty and perfidy; but of having made ourselves liable to all punishments which follow upon such sins—to arbitrary punishment at the hands of any civilized nation who might see fit to call us to account, and to that more certain natural

[106] Helen M. Hunt, *A Century of Dishonour: A Sketch of the United States Government's Dealings with some of the North American Tribes* (London: Chatto & Windus, Piccadilly, 1881), 27-9

> punishment which, sooner or later, as surely comes from evil-doing as harvests from sown seed.[107]

Even in the late-nineteenth century, many Americans aware of the government's dealings with Native American tribes realized that the U.S. was already involved with foreign relations or treaties. The situation with Mexico—i.e. the annexation of Texas (1845) and the vast land area gained from the 1848 Treaty of Guadalupe Hidalgo at the end of the Mexican-American War (1846-48)—was a similar example. Just because the land territories in question—parts of Arizona, New Mexico, Colorado, and Nevada, Utah, California, and Texas—are today part of the United States does not mean that they "naturally" are; to argue that they are naturally part of the U.S. is to promote the ideology of Manifest Destiny. This argument applies clearly to the removal of the Five Civilized Tribes from their native lands in the South to Indian Territory after the Indian Removal Act of 1830.

Despite the general trends, of railroads, wars, and treaties, the actual settlement of Palestine and the North American interior was the result of individuals' decisions. The settlers to Indian Territory and Palestine were not forced to go there. Consequently, it may make more sense to define nationalism as the sum of social pressures that create a sort of common or imagined unity of peoples. On a personal level, nationalisms or ideologies rest on the decisions of individuals who consciously chose to identify themselves within the categories of unity and difference—e.g., adopting a specific lifestyle as a means to fit in with a specific sort of society, and thus also with the nation that supported said society. What was really important to many Americans and Zionists (regardless of ethnicity/race) was just living a life with a decent standard of living; they chose to re-define themselves to fit what they believed to represent the prevailing lifestyle.

Strong belief, whether based on ideals, like the ideologies of Zionism and Manifest Destiny discussed in this chapter, or symbols like modernism (the topic of the next

---

[107] Ibid. 29.

chapter), was the life blood of nationalism. A collection of many individuals expressing belief in an ideal or symbol was enough to bring it into being in solid, material form in their community. Zionism took physical, material form as the city of Tel Aviv. Manifest Destiny took solid, material form as the city of Tulsa.

Chapter Four

Symbols

Tropes of Urban Space

"Social relations have no real existence save in space. Their underpinning is spatial. In each particular case, the connection between this underpinning and the relations it supports calls for analysis" and "a critique of those institutions" and other factors "that have transformed the space under consideration."[108] According to Henri Lefebvre, space gives meaning to the underlying economic, political, and social structures that comprise both urban areas and society at large. Cities such as Tel Aviv and Tulsa, with clear histories of land-dispossession in order to create modernist European-style settlements, are clear examples of Lefebvre's theory. Architecture, urban planning, and western concepts of land settlement and development became tools of conquest in contested frontier areas like Palestine and Indian Territory. Establishing new cities—of which Tel Aviv and Tulsa were the most successful and important—created the essential foothold that European-Zionist and American settlers needed. The urban settlements of Tel Aviv and Tulsa allowed the newcomers to create the narrative that their urban development patterns were both justified and flourishing. Therefore, Tulsa and Tel Aviv were built on modernist myths. The city elites and officials promoted development projects and a "culture" in line with their definition of what a modern city was like. This meant specific architecture types, specific types of urban plans, new sanitary codes, and a specific way of talking about their city in public and to the press.

Tulsa, like Tel Aviv, was ground zero of the struggle for land in the "frontier" area at the forefront of interaction and competition between Europeans or Americans and non-European-descended indigenous peoples. Tulsa and Tel Aviv were both explicitly modern settlements, and cities, established by the self-styled civilized European-

[108] Henri Lefebvre, *The Production of Space,* translated by Donald Nicholson-Smith (Hoboken, NJ: Wiley-Blackwell, 1992), 404.

descended newcomers who, by building a modern-style city in the "desert," hoped to create a "city on the sands" or a "magic city."[109]

A common feature of the ideological framework behind these cities' settlement was the trope of the modern and the traditional, or civilized and backward; this trope played a central role in facilitating and justifying European and American colonialist, imperialist policies—and ultimately was central to the founding myths of Tel Aviv and Tulsa. This framework has been fleshed out more clearly by scholars of the Middle East than of the United States—but, I am suggesting that the general ideas and framework fits Tulsa just as well as Tel Aviv.

The binary framework of modern versus traditional presented "modern" cities as having European-influenced architecture, wide streets, and technological developments such as street lighting and improved sanitation, and a secularized public sphere. In contrast, the framework identified the "traditional" city in the Middle East as having winding and narrow streets, and lacking in technological refinements (like electricity and modern sewers). The net result of such analysis, carried out by scholars of European/American training, was that the 'West" came to represent secular progress while the "East" came to represent nations less civilized than Europe. One of the first books to critically/intellectually examine the unequal power of this relationship was Edward Said's 1978 book *Orientalism.* Said revolutionized the intellectual framework for examining European perceptions of the Middle East. Said showed how nineteenth-century writers recycled the earlier descriptions of the "East"--for example, Edward Lane's drawing from Gerard de Nerval--to create a self-generating framework emphasizing the "otherness" of the Middle East that has continued to the present day. Said was thus one of the first to recognize and problematize the binary framework of modern versus traditional.

Analyzing the interplay between modern versus traditional urban development is not a simple matter of describing structural changes, because as recent scholarship has emphasized, this binary framework grew out of and perpetuates the unfounded ideology that "progressive" European nations modernized "traditional" (and implied not-

---

[109] The words in quotes were all commonly used by Zionist and American settlers of Tel Aviv and Tulsa.

progressive) nations in the Middle East. There are two issues here: the first is analyzing the nature of modernity and modernization, which is a problematic framework even without the added complications of the colonial context, and the second is how to recover local perspectives and cultural/social vitality from this framework's fore-fronting of European dominance and colonial control. Consequently, some recent scholars have sought to drop this binary altogether, and find less-charged terminology.

Tel Aviv is a city commonly described as a product of European Imperialism, where the Israelis (Zionists) took over Palestinian-Arab land (best symbolized by Jaffa). As a colonial city, shaped by Ottoman, British, and Zionist influence, Tel Aviv's modern image necessitated the ideological and physical clearing of existing development. To that end, despite the continual struggles with the neighboring and ancient Arab-controlled city of Jaffa, Tel Aviv consistently but fraudulently portrayed itself as a frontier outpost built upon undeveloped sands, and thus a city with a clean slate and no ties to the past. Architecture played a central role in this self-image, as Tel Aviv's Zionist founders embraced modern city planning and architecture as an explicit counter to their perception of Jaffa as old-fashioned, dirty, unplanned, and full of violent Arabs.

Tulsa, however, has not been described in such unambiguous terms. Yet, in many ways, Tulsa has a very similar history to Tel Aviv. Outlining those similarities is one contribution of this book.

One of the reasons that Tulsa has not been studied in detail as a colonial, or post-colonial, city is because the United States does not choose to recognize its spread westward across North America as anything but the manifest destiny of the nation achieving its natural borders. Of course, to view the Native American tribes that occupied the land now occupied by the U.S. as legitimate nations as the U.S. Congress officially did prior to 1871 (which was when the U.S. Congress "either ashamed of making treaties only to break them, or grudging the time, money and paper it wasted, passed an act to the effect that no Indian tribe should hereafter be considered as a foreign nation with whom the

United States might contract a treaty")[110] would mean that the U.S. forcibly conquered the indigenous nations and subsumed their lands into the territory of the United States. In the mid-nineteenth century, the United States was an imperialist nation in all but name because its spread westward meant conquering independent indigenous nations in order to create U.S. territories and, over time, states.

The common argument is that the United States' control of the Americas, including its manifest destiny or westward spread across North America south of Canada, was different from European colonial or imperial systems because it was largely recognized as a valid part of U.S. territory by European nations after the Louisiana Purchase (with exceptions, of course, such disputes over the boundaries of the Louisiana Territory). This only makes the connections with Palestine clearer: the only nations who stood in the United States' way were the indigenous peoples; in the land area of the Louisiana Purchase, as in Palestine, the native people were regarded by Americans and Europeans as non-civilized and so largely irrelevant. Emphasizing the modernist style of development as civilizing the "frontier" was the key to sustaining Tulsa and Tel Aviv's booster myth.

Tel Aviv

When the European-based Zionists came to Palestine, they saw Jaffa as an old-fashioned and backward city, despite the fact that by the time of the arrival of the first Zionists in the late-nineteenth century, Jaffa was already "modernizing" on its own initiative.

The Bazaar, Jaffa, 1896-1914

[110] Helen M. Hunt, *A Century of Dishonour: A Sketch of the United States Government's Dealings with some of the North American Tribes* (London: Chatto & Windus, Piccadilly, 1881), 27.

In the mid-nineteenth century, Ottoman authorities turned to modernization as a solution to specific problems with the existing norms. Rebuilding logically took on a more European fashion, as local authorities took measures to build wider and straighter streets and attempted to showcase monuments. The Ottoman Empire was keenly aware of the political implications of urban space, and chose specific architectural styles to establish geographically defined administrative centers within their cities to symbolically demonstrate their political authority. In other words, architectural representation both created and legitimated government authority, so the Ottomans wanted to modernize based on the newest technology-based European models. For this reason, there was a marked contrast between the crowded and less affluent neighborhoods of the Old City and newer and wealthier outlying section—of which Tel Aviv is only one example--built in the new European style and utilizing recent technological developments. Geographical divisions between sections of the same urban area provide a revealing snapshot of how the modern/traditional split also reflected class divisions and competition between urban/suburban areas.

Fishermen at Jaffa

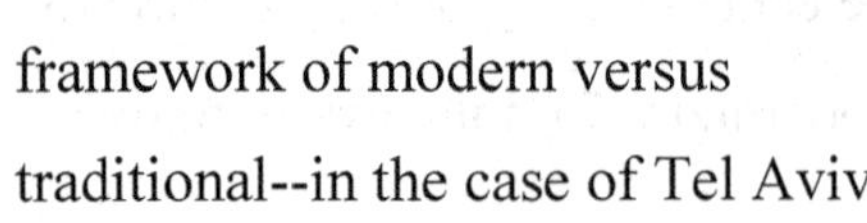

Most significantly, talk of modern versus tradition was a means for European newcomers like the Zionists to self-identify as more progressive, civilized, and therefore more-deserving of settling and developing the land. The binary framework of modern versus traditional--in the case of Tel Aviv and Jaffa—is a myth the Zionists promoted to present themselves as superior to the Arabs on the basis of their more-European style of architecture and city-building; that is why they ignored the modernization of Jaffa's architecture and infrastructure that had begun before the establishment of Tel Aviv.

Buildings under construction, 1930

Despite its rapid growth into a bustling city, Tel Aviv maintained its official commitment to Zionism. For example, at a 25-year anniversary celebration for Tel Aviv's founding, the speakers admonished: "the wonderful economic development of the town in the economic field must be paralleled by cultural development," because of "the danger threatening the city if its cultural life is neglected."[111] In 1931, the Palestine Bulletin published an editorial that succinctly described Tel Aviv's positive self-image as a multifaceted, globally significant place—significant primarily because it was the largest modern and Zionist Hebrew city. Tel Aviv's boosters delighted in proclaiming the city's myths: "a sand patch" that had become a flourishing "city of Jews"; a place "built mostly by the poor in worldly goods, rich in spirit"; a "city of artists" and "city of poets" with many "book-shops, printers, publishers"; and a "city of small industries." These statements often bordered on grandiosity, of which many Tel Avivi were aware but defiant: "To the critical and unsympathetic Tel Aviv may seem not at all that its lovers claim for it. They may not see the divine flash of creativeness that lights up the whole town. They may wonder how the Mayor can dream of such a town as this becoming a City of God." Tel Aviv may have seemed "deceptive" for outsiders to understand, but "from inside," in light of "what it means to those who have built" Tel Aviv, it seemed obvious that Tel Aviv was everything locals said it was and more.[112]

Statistics supporting Tel Aviv's self-proclaimed modernity included: its municipal public library had 25,000 volumes; international banks like Great Britain's Barclays Bank had offices in Tel Aviv; Tel Aviv's streets were wired for electricity ten years before

[111] "Tel Aviv's Birthday," *The Palestine Post*, May 07, 1943, page 1.
[112] "Pebbles on the Beach of Tel Aviv," *The Palestine Bulletin*, March 02, 1931, page 5.

Jerusalem's were; the city had a "highly adequate bus service"; and the finest meteorological station in Palestine was located in the city. In addition, Tel Aviv was almost-completely a Jewish city, as "not more than 10 Christians" and only "40 Moslems" lived there, out of the 1931 population of 50,000. Tel Aviv was also a city of artists and high culture: "No other town in the world with so small a population boasts so many artists" and Tel Aviv had the only local art museum in all of Palestine. Moreover, Tel Aviv had two daily Hebrew-language newspapers, as well as "seven weeklies, one fort-nightly, two monthlies, one quarterly and countless occasional publications produced in Tel Aviv," and "those claiming to be authors and journalists number nearly 200."[113]

A Factory in Tel Aviv, c. 1925-1940

Tel Aviv promoted its industrial growth, as a means of illustrating its modernity. City boosters claimed Tel Aviv was on pace to be a major industrial city; for example, in 1933 "The industrial growth of Tel Aviv proceeds apace and new openings are constantly being explored. One of these is metal products, the manufacture of which will be undertaken by the Barzalit company, which has fully paid up share capital of LP. 10,000." This company sought to produce "wire-netting of all kinds" at its "modern factory" in Tel Aviv that would employ "eighty workmen."[114]

Tel Aviv Industries, c. 1925-1940

Many of the Zionists, including David Ben-Gurion, Israel's first Prime Minister, represented the Labor Party and were deeply influenced by socialism. During the 1920s

[113] "Tel Aviv," *The Palestine Bulletin,* March 02, 1931, page 2.
[114] "New Metal Works in Tel Aviv," *The Palestine Post*, June 07, 1933, page 5.

and 1930s—the time of Tel Aviv's maturation into a city instead of a "suburb" of Jaffa—a photography campaign was undertaken to document Tel Aviv's happy industrial workers.

The most successful development project in pre-Israeli-independence Tel Aviv was the completion of Tel Aviv Port in the 1930s, as competition for Jaffa Port. "The all-Jewish port at Tel Aviv achieved a status of equality with the Haifa and Jaffa harbors when the Palestine government informed the Jewish Agency for Palestine that Tel Aviv had been included among the ports permitted to handle the export of citrus fruit." This was significant because Jaffa's main international export was oranges. As of July 1936, "Millions of cases of such fruit have been shipped annually from Haifa and Jaffa"; now Tel Aviv would be able to cut into that lucrative market, as "Ships are now proceeding directly to Tel Aviv, receiving free license to dock there, instead of stopping at Jaffa as previously."[115] Escalating violence between Jews and Arabs in 1936 encouraged the British High Commissioner to relocate "certain Government administrative offices" to Tel Aviv, which would now "function independently of Jaffa" in the Tel Aviv Municipality; these administrative offices included the department of the District Office, the Revenue and Stamps offices, and the

Tel Aviv Port, 1938

[115] "Wider Recognition for Tel Aviv Port," *The Sentinel,* July 30, 1936, page 33.

Licenses Bureau.[116] Tel Aviv proceeded to build a walled border between it and Jaffa—with Manshiya as part of the boundary area--but the border remained porous.

Through 1938 Tel Aviv Port and Jaffa Port had shared tonnage of ships docked in port to export and import cargo, but in 1939 Tel Aviv Port began a campaign to force Tel Avivi to exclusively use Tel Aviv Port. In October 1939 Tel Aviv's mayor, shipping-company representatives, and the Emergency Supply Committee, Chamber of Commerce, and the Emergency Committee for Port Affairs and the Management of the Port met and decided to mandate "the use of Tel Aviv Port for the landing of all imports consigned to the city."[117] The officially stated purpose of this policy was "not…to compete with Haifa" or with Jaffa, but to ensure the success of Tel Aviv's own port; therefore, the Tel Aviv Port Committee (based on the October 1939 agreement) announced it would fine all companies or individuals from Tel Aviv bypassing Tel Aviv Port.[118]

Urban sprawl—the spreading out of urbanized development patterns well beyond municipal boundaries—led to rapid growth of surrounding suburban settlements. In 1934, for example, Tel Aviv's expansion spawned its "newest suburb," Givath Rambam (named after Maimonides), which "is situated on an elevation, commanding a fine view of the sea and Jaffa, Tel Aviv and of their suburbs;" Zionist Jews had purchased this 250 dunam settlement (roughly 62 acres) after ten years of negotiation.[119] Zionists during the pre-Israel decades (i.e., pre-1948) sought to obtain land by purchasing it from individuals like absentee Arab landowners; the early Zionist settlements including Tel Aviv (as Ahuzat Bayit in 1909) had all been purchased through such negotiation.

---

[116] "Government Offices for Tel Aviv," *The Palestine Post,* May 21, 1936, page 7.
[117] "Ship through Tel Aviv Port," *The Palestine Post,* October 23, 1939, page 2.
[118] "Protecting Tel Aviv's Port," *The Palestine Post*, November 06, 1939.
[119] "Tel Aviv's Newest Suburb," *The Palestine Post,* July 11, 1934, page 5.

Buses and autos in Tel Aviv, 1930s

The continued growth of the Jaffa-Tel Aviv metropolitan area, had by the 1930s, caused problems of traffic congestion, as many residents in the city and suburbs purchased automobiles and trucks. All across Palestine, automobile sales were burgeoning, and even growing exponentially.[120] Despite the rising numbers of car and truck owners, bus transit was a primary means of transportation; in the month of July in 1934 the municipality of Tel Aviv determined that 1,700,000 passengers had ridden city buses--operated by the Hamaavir Company—for an average of 5,000 passengers per day. Due to such high demand and road congestion, wait times were long and passengers were often forced to "wait a full hour for a bus."[121] In 1934-1935, Tel Aviv's traffic was "about ten times as heavy as that in Berlin." In "Tel Aviv there is one vehicle to every twenty persons," including "1,662 autos and 2,013 horse drawn conveyances" as well as "6,070 omnibuses, motorcycles and vans."[122] In 1938 Tel Aviv attempted to improve and consolidate its bus service by announcing an official design competition for plans for building a new "Central Autobus Station in Tel Aviv."[123] This process culminated in the

[120] Auto ownership in Palestine nearly doubled in 1934 from roughly 6000 to 10,189 autos, and experts expected a "similar increase" in 1935 as well. "Palestine Motor Traffic," *The Palestine Post,* December 03, 1935, page 2.

[121] "Congestion in Tel Aviv," *The Palestine Post,* August 10, 1934, page 5.

[122] "Tel Aviv's Traffic Heavier than Berlin's." *The Sentinel,* March 21, 1935 page 11.

[123] "Municipal Corporation of Tel Aviv," *The Palestine Post*, October 21, 1938, page 9.

1941 opening of the Central Bus Station in the Jewish neighborhood of Neve Sha'anan (est. 1921, annexed by Tel Aviv in 1927) in the southeastern part of the city.

Tel Aviv's most disappointing public works project may be the New Central Bus Station, begun in the 1960s near the site of the 1941 Central Bus Station in the Neve Sha'anan area. Buses have historically been Tel Aviv's primary means of public transport within city limits, but the New Central Bus Station was a disaster; construction began in 1967, but was delayed for decades due to financial problems, and work was not completed until 1993. The project was the brainchild of an entrepreneur, Arieh Piltz, who began buying up lots in the area in 1960, and was pushed through by Tel Aviv's major bus companies: Solel Boneh, Egged, and Piltz. Yet, the station plan "was completely at odds with the expert advice offered by planners" because "Tel Aviv was naturally linear in form, clearly lacked a centre and therefore had no use for a 'central' station."[124] The decades-long delay proved that the planners, not the bus companies, were correct.

Tel Aviv also invested in rail transit. The HaTachana station (built in 1892 and also called Jaffa Railway Station) in the Manshiya-Neve Tzedek area was still open (until 1948), but Tel Aviv planners sought a newer station. In 1937, Tel Aviv planners debated the location of a new station; construction began on a site outside of city limits, near the Petah Tikva road (today's Begin Road) in the north-eastern area of Tel Aviv. However, in a March 1937 meeting representatives of the Tel Aviv "Municipality requested that the station should be built within the city limits and a site in Rehov Herzl and Nahlat Benjamin" in the center of the city "or at the corner of Rehov Harakevet" (translated as Railway Street) east of downtown, which corresponded more closely with the existing Tel Aviv South Railway Station's location near the Petah Tikva Road;[125] however, it took several decades before this new station (Tel Aviv North) was completed. Israeli independence led to a flurry of railroad-station construction. Tel Aviv North opened in 1949 at the intersection of Tel Aviv and the neighboring municipalities of Bnei Brak and Ramat Gan. This station supplanted the existing rail line from the north-east towns, a roundabout rail spur that had been constructed to connect the railway station in Rosh

[124] Sharon Rotbard, *White City, Black City,* 149.
[125] "Tel Aviv Passenger Railway Station," *The Palestine Post,* March 03, 1937, page 7.

HaAyin to Jaffa, via the area towns of Petah Tikva and Lod in order to transport citrus fruit from area orchards to Jaffa Port. But the Tel Aviv North Station remained far away from Tel Aviv proper; today, it has been redeveloped and rebuilt as Bnei Brak Station. Another important development was the beginning of passenger rail service in 1949 and expanded to "Saturday nights and Close of Holidays" (because Saturday is Shabbat observance, there was no daytime service) in April 1950 between Tel Aviv and Haifa;[126] at first, trains on this line went to Rosh South station before heading into Jaffa, but in the early 1950s the HaYarkon Railroad Station was built. In 1954, the new Tel Aviv Center railway station, located in north-eastern Tel Aviv near the Ayalon River, and located in the middle area between of the lanes of the Ayalon Expressway, became Tel Aviv's new primary station. The Tel Aviv Center station was originally the terminus of the Coastal railway line, which only ran trains to the north (toward Haifa), although in the 1980s it was updated as Tel Aviv Savidor Central Railway Station and now runs trains in all directions throughout the metropolitan region.

Despite all these public works projects, Tel Aviv faced serious environmental and pollution problems by the late 1930s, many of which would continue for decades and even up to the present day. In 1939, for example, Y. Shiffman, Tel Aviv's municipal engineer, explained that Tel Aviv's continuing infrastructure problems were because "the city has been faced with difficulties unknown elsewhere." Tel Aviv's population by 1939—which was prior to the huge post-World War Two immigration surge--"has expanded tenfold in twenty years, its area has grown haphazardly and outrageous prices have had to be paid for land; its citizens have had to provide for all the civic amenities which elsewhere are spread over several generations."[127]

Sanitation had been one of the first issues the British Mandate government addressed after 1917, when they took control of Palestine. The Public Health Ordinance of 1918 included provisions to improve sanitation and guard against the spread of infectious disease; this ordinance prevented the spread of infectious disease with measures such as requiring government notification of deaths and of illness, mandated vaccinations

---

[126] "Timetable for Passenger Trains on the Haifa-Tel Aviv Line," *The Palestine Post,* April 210, 1950, page 3.

[127] "Tenfold in 20 Years," *The Palestine Post,* August 07, 1939, page 5.

(especially for children), and setting standards for licensing medical officers and doctors.[128] Likewise--since animal carcasses were a primary waste of the period--in 1926, and updated in 1930, the British-Mandate government implemented the Diseases of Animals Ordinance to require specific standards for disposing of the carcass of any animal that died of disease.[129] The British Mandate and the Israeli (post-1948) governments continued to implement new sanitary ordinances as needed over the following decades, but problems remained.

By 1960, many impoverished residents of Tel Aviv were dissatisfied with the unsanitary nature of the city. People decried the vast amounts of garbage and litter associated with Tel Aviv's vibrant commercial establishments, and argued for the need for street cleaning machines and new disposal bins on city streets.[130] Impoverished immigrants often lived next to dumpsites, and Tel Aviv relied on Arabs and recent immigrants for much of its sanitation work, which intensified tensions. In 1964, for example, Tel Aviv-Yafo's sanitation workers struck "over a pay increase they claimed had been promised them"; in response, the Tel Aviv Municipality decided to "send out loud speakers ahead of its garbage vans and ask residents to dump their refuse themselves into the trucks."[131] In Tel Aviv-Yafo, the affluent and newer areas in the north were cleaner and better serviced by the city, but southern Tel Aviv (Jaffa, Manshiya, and the first Jewish neighborhoods) "just grew—or was planned so haphazardly that it should be razed at once. There are still slums full of dilapidated shacks, cabins, and shanties. Their streets are only narrow alleys; often not paved, and generally used for sewers."[132] Whereas the municipality focused on new technology and proclaimed it had everything under control, low-income residents argued that behind the "pretentious language" the reality was that Tel Aviv was

---

[128] Government of Palestine, *Legislation of Palestine 1918-1925,* compiled by Norman Bentwich, (Alexandria, Egypt: Whitehead Morris, 1926), 45-50.
[129] *Diseases of Animals Ordinance*, 1926 and revised in 1930. Government of Palestine, *Proclamations, Regulations, Rules, Orders and Notices: Annual Volume for 1930* (Jerusalem, IL: Greek Convent Press), 347-9.
[130] A 1960 report lamented the "unhappy fact that, only a few hours after municipal street sweeps finish their work, the streets are already littered with paper and all kinds of refuse." See "Sanitation Situation Must Be Improved: Public Cooperation Essential," *The Jerusalem Post*, May 13, 1960.
[131] "Hunger Strike Gains Jobs," *The Jerusalem Post,* August 21, 1964.
[132] Macabee Dean, "Mechanical means to 'keep cities clean," *The Jerusalem Post,* 1964.

a "smelly and polluted city."[133] This distance between the positions of the municipality and many residents showed the holes in the municipality's "progress through technology" narrative.

Pollution was an overarching concern in Tel Aviv-Yafo in the 1960s. In 1961, the Knesset (Israel's Parliament) passed the Abatement of Nuisances Law in order to address air, odor, and noise pollution. Israeli courts, however, were loath to interpret the law as binding, and often refused to grant standing to persons and groups seeking to utilize it as the basis for legal action.[134] Therefore, there was little legal basis at this time to force the municipality of Tel Aviv-Yafo to take specific action that it was not otherwise inclined to take. In the 1960s air pollution was on the rise: general sources such as automobiles and fires as well as a site-specific source--the Reading D power station--were the main culprits; environmental historians commonly cite the late-1960s expansion of the Reading D power plant as the major watershed of the environmental movement in Tel Aviv.[135] The Hiriya (חירייה) garbage dump and the old Mikve Israel dump both spawned several fires, billowing black smoke, which added to the sense that Tel Aviv's sanitation needed serious improvement.[136] The deterioration of the city's waterfront and rivers was another serious environmental issue. Tel Aviv was a major tourist attraction for its beaches, yet the beachfront had been "allowed to degenerate in many parts to an odious rubbish dump," and the city's sewage pipes were too short, so they commonly spewed raw sewage along the beachfront.[137] In 1961 Tel Aviv began a project to increase the length of the pipes from 50 to 150 meters off shore to over 800 meters; in 1963, plans were underway to "establish a sewage purification transferred through pumps and correcting

[133] "Emergency Tel Aviv!," *Herut*, August 24, 1964.
[134]"Administrative Cases Under Judicial Order: Oppenheimer $ ors. v. Ministers of Interior and Health," *Israel Law Review,* 1 (1966): 462-506.
[135] "Technology expert: Split power plant will not prevent air pollution in North Tel Aviv," *Davar*, December 10, 1967; "The decision regarding Reading," *Davar*, March 25, 1968; Avraham Rotem, "Reading D 'pollution unchecked,' *Maariv*, July 01, 1970; "Control Commission offers urban Reading" *Davar*, July 08, 1970; "In the shadow of the chimney," *Davar*, August 06, 1970.
[136]: Oded Zarai, "Air pollution over the skies of Tel Aviv," *Herut*, May 23, 1961. Jerusalem Post Reporter, "1 Death, Heavy Damage in T.A. Fire," September 25, 1962; "Garbage Dump Still Burning in Tel Aviv," *The Jerusalem Post*, September 27, 1962.
[137] Paul Kohn, "Tel Aviv Seafront Is in Sorry State," *The Jerusalem Post* May 18, 1962. No Author listed, "Doctors beachcombing, Tel Aviv," *Davar*, June, 30, 1955. Nangi Magac, "Where washed up this year?" *Davar*, May 28, 1957; Acraf Rots, "Prosecutors to take action against marine pollution in Tel Aviv," *Maariv*, June 22, 1968; "Shape of the beach area of Tel Aviv will change completely within 3 years," *Davar*, June 02, 1969; "Beaches closed today," *Maariv*, October 15, 1974.

Tel Aviv bathing beach, 1940s

crushing solids" to carry sewage "to sea in the tube, will keep the sewage 800 meters from the beach."[138] The heavy pollution of Tel Aviv's rivers--especially the Yarkon River, which emptied into the sea at the city's northern limit—was a similarly disastrous pollution concern.[139]

Despite the aforementioned concern for the growing environmental problems in Tel Aviv, the official stance was that modernization and industrial development was positive. Therefore, Israel's general policy focus was on encouraging development, not on environmental issues such as abating pollution. In 1965, Israel implemented the Planning and Building Law.[140] This was a comprehensive statute to monitor and regulate "all building and land use designations in Israel." This law created "a hierarchy of planning bodies (national, regional, and local) responsible for land-use planning, taking into consideration all potential impacts, including environmental impacts." Israeli legislation largely favored industry, however, and in practice environmentalist groups--like Malraz (the Council for the Prevention of Noise and Air pollution in Israel) in its fight against Tel Aviv's proposed Reading Power Station in 1968—"had little legal power."[141]

Tel Aviv's focus on progress through development was an essential aspect of its self-professed modernity. In order to perpetuate this myth, Tel Aviv's elites and

---

[138] "Sewage program changes in the Dan Region," *Davar*, April 11, 1955.

[139] See, for example: Fofed Defrahaysor, "City of Tel-Aviv-Jaffa Hayarkon pollution alerts on water-waste," *Davar*, December 06, 1964. This article describes a local Tel Aviv protest movement to stop the flow of raw sewage from "water drainage of communities far from Tel-Aviv through wadis to the Yarkon River, which will lead to contamination of the river." See also Avraham Rotem, "Give fish to Yarkon River," *Maariv*, June 24, 1970.

[140] Planning and Building Law, 5725-1965.

[141] Ariel Bin-Nun, *The Law of the State of Israel: An Introduction* (Jerusalem: Ruben Mass Ltd., 1990), 96.

policymakers had to willfully ignore large sections of the city—especially the more-impoverished areas of the south. Symbolically, Jaffa and the southern neighborhoods are "everything hidden by the long, dark shadow of the White City" of Tel Aviv's UNESCO-sanctioned Bauhaus-style lore; the Jaffa area is "everything Tel Aviv does not see and everything it does not want to see."[142] Tel Aviv's myth of modernity is based on perpetuating the Zionist ideals at the expense of everyday reality.

Tulsa

Tulsa emphasized its modernity as well, at the cost of erasure. Its main narrative was enterprising economic, industrial, and civic growth, as the means of achieving modernity.

Tulsa's Frisco Railroad

From the beginning, Tulsa's elites were concerned with promoting the newly constructed city as modern. Railroads, banking, oil, and consumer goods—merchants, general stores—were the reasons Tulsa became a city. These industries and occupations all had a vested interest in ensuring Tulsa's continued emphasis on progress through modern means. J.M. Hall, who came to Tulsa in 1882 to work on the railroad spur with his brother H.C. Hall, was one of Tulsa's prominent merchants and bankers. In his book *The Beginning of Tulsa* Hall emphasized the role of the railroads as "the vein through which the town's life blood flowed."[143]

The Frisco, or St. Louis and San Francisco Railroad (completed in Tulsa in 1882) was only the first of many to reach downtown Tulsa. In 1902, Tulsa's Commercial Club of elite, wealthy citizens convinced the Missouri, Kansas, and Texas—known as the Katy--

[142] Sharon Rotbard, *White City, Black City*, 66.
[143] James Monroe Hall, *The Beginning of Tulsa* (Tulsa, c. 1933), 9.

railway line to alter its original plan to bypass Tulsa several miles to the east and instead re-route through central Tulsa. In 1903, Tulsa was able to convince the Midland Valley Railroad to go through Tulsa. Likewise, the Santa Fe Railway completed its track through Tulsa as well. Tulsa's last railroad was a local-service track built by Charles Page, a Tulsa oilman, after he established the Sand Springs Home for orphans and widows; the Sand Springs Railway "created one of Tulsa's major transportation corridors" and linked Tulsa with the oil fields west of the Arkansas River.[144]

Streetcar in downtown, 1909

Much of Tulsa's early growth was based on its railroad networks, which opened it up as a central destination for cattle drives. Its major railroad companies had reached Tulsa before the oil boom of the Glenn Pool transformed Tulsa. Tulsa's existing railroads, however, enabled it to become the premier petroleum-industry center in the area. The money that flowed into Tulsa after the discovery of the Glenn Pool and of subsequent oil fields was made possible because of the railroad lines linking much of Indian Territory or Oklahoma to Tulsa.

With the rise of the automobile in the 1910s and 1920s, Tulsa expanded its road infrastructure to accommodate this new form of transportation. Tulsa had lots of open space and room for growth, and paved streets built on the grid system--with a major thoroughfare roughly marking every square mile--soon crisscrossed the city. Financing for Tulsa's new roads came from local bond issues, as Oklahoma's state government was divided over the issue of state-funded roads.[145]

---

[144] "Transportation (1850-1945), Tulsa Preservation Commission, http://tulsapreservationcommission.org/tulsa-history/transportation/ , Accessed January 2017.
[145] "Oklahoma: The Early Years," *Tulsa Tribune,* no date, page 13.

Streetcars were also common in downtown Tulsa, as well as links connecting downtown and various neighborhoods. In 1909, competition between Tulsa's two streetcar companies, Tulsa Street Railway (TSR) and Oklahoma Union Traction Company (OUT) reached a summit of the "hectic races" for political favor and popular votes "to see which company would gain new trackage." In the short term, both companies succeeded, as Tulsa's Commercial Club and voters approved funds for both.[146] Streetcar lines were widespread in center-city streets and are clearly visible in photographs from the early 1920s.

5th St. and Main, c. 1921

Tulsa's streetcar system began as "a bargaining chip" used by land developer Grant C. Stebbins to convince Kendall College—now The University of Tulsa—to relocate from its campus in Muskogee. In 1905 the Tulsa municipality passed the ordinance to create the TSR. In 1909 TSR operated streetcars on "Main Street from 10th to Cameron and down Frisco to 15th, the site of the residential Sophian Plaza. Other routes traveled along North Cheyenne to the Fairgrounds, The University of Tulsa and several points between." Meanwhile, OUT streetcars connected downtown to Orcutt Park and Swan Lake. As was common in North American cities, new housing developments sprung up along the routes. By 1923, TSR "had 21 miles of track and 52 cars. The banner year of 1916 showed a profit of over $1.2 million by 2010 standards but the advent of World War I, and its resulting inflation, were a blow to the intra-city trolley lines." Therefore, TSR folded in 1926 and OUT ended its service in 1935.[147]

[146] "Early day Transportation Systems Feudin', Fightin'," *Tulsa Tribune*, November 07, 1949.
[147] Steve Gerkin, "Electric to Eco Trolley: Champions of Tulsa Transportation," *This Land*, 08/20/2011. http://thislandpress.com/2011/08/20/electric-to-eco-trolley-champions-of-tulsa-transportation/?read=complete. Accessed January 2017.

One of the most important aspects of Tulsa's economic and industrial diversification was aviation. From the 1920s through the 1940s, Tulsa was an aviation pioneer city, due in large part to its oil-rich residents. William G. (Bill) Skelly was the founder of Spartan Aeronautics in 1928, but in 1935 he ceded control to Jean Paul Getty, and Getty took personal control of Spartan's programs in 1942. Under Getty's leadership, Spartan developed into a military-airplane manufacturer during World War Two, and expanded its Spartan School, which since 1943 has offered degrees in many fields of flight and aviation-related engineering. Soon after Spartan opened, on January 27, 1928, Tulsa's opened its municipal airport: on July 3, 1928. By 1929, there were four airports in Tulsa: the McIntyre, H. F. Wilcox, Garland, and North American Airlines fields. In 1929, Tulsa also had two airplane manufacturers: Collier Aircraft, based at Wilcox airport, and Spartan, located next to the municipal airport. In 1936 American Airlines included Tulsa in its routes, and established a permanent manufacturing facility in Tulsa in December 1945; "American Airlines took possession of the former Douglas Aircraft's modification plant, reopening it on June 1, 1946. This became one of the nation's largest maintenance bases, but it had already begun operations in January 1941 when Douglas was awarded a contract to build for World War II production."[148]

First Interstate Freight Shipment by Air, 1919

Gas Station converted to a bar, 1942

Tulsa's economy remained strong. Railroads in Tulsa continued to play a significant role in the city's oil and petroleum industry. During World War Two, Tulsa's railroads and Great Lakes Pipeline supplied to the war effort, and brought prosperity to Tulsa. This pipeline was "a common carrier of refined petroleum products such as diesel fuel, heating oil, and gasoline," to carry

[148] Carl E. Gregory, "Tulsa," Accessed November 2016.

Tulsa's petroleum products to the northern Midwest: Kansas City, Des Moines, Minneapolis, and into North Dakota.[149] Nevertheless, oil rations within Tulsa—as across the Unites States--were strictly enforced, and many petrol stations in Tulsa were converted to other uses, such as a bar. Tulsa's petrochemical industries never quite reached the level of the 1920s, but World War Two did provide a needed boost to the city's economy.

Oil Cars on the Frisco RR, 1942

After World War Two, Tulsa's petrochemical focus gave way to a broader spectrum of corporations. Tulsa was typical of Sunbelt cities during the postwar decades: Tulsa's pleasant climate and lax labor regulations attracted diverse corporations relocating from the Rustbelt states of the northeast and upper Midwest.

After World War Two, Tulsa continued to expand its high-speed highways. This was a nation-wide trend, backed by federal funds, based in part on the reasoning that an extensive network of highways, expressways, and parkways would connect the urban center with the expanding suburbs while cementing the center's hold as the

Tulsa Postcard, c. 1965

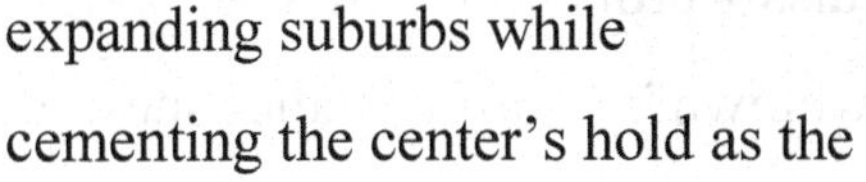

149 William B. Fredericks, *In the Long Haul: The Life of John Raun* (Iowa City: The University of Iowa Press), 37.

primary destination for white-collar work, shopping, and entertainment. In reality, building expressways furthered growth away from the central city areas, leading to a decline of the downtown and inner-city areas. Offices, shopping centers, and

Mural of Tulsa's Petroleum Origins, 1966

entertainment venues began relocating to the outer core of cities, often along the expressways, which led city officials to call for building more expressways to serve the growing amount of traffic. Tulsa became a city where transportation was based on individual automobiles and a municipal bus service. In October 1957 voters in Tulsa "approved a bond issue to finance a modern Expressway System in the Tulsa Metropolitan area." This program, expected to cost in excess of fifty-million dollars, "justifies this belief" that "Tulsa's growth over the next 50 years should be even greater than during the past 50 years" when Tulsa grew from "an Indian Territory town of 7,298 population in 1907 to a modern city of over 250,000."[150]

In the late 1960s, Tulsa's planners decided to build the Crosstown Expressway (today's Interstate 244) through north Tulsa, linking Interstate 44 (which traveled through the southern part of the city) via a bypass directly with downtown. Since first beginning the planning process for new expressways in the 1940s, "Tulsa's problem was how to build an expressway across the city so that it would serve downtown"; "Traffic studies showed

[150] A.E Bradshaw and W.A. Brownlee, "National Bank of Tulsa Annual Report: Planning Ahead With Tulsa," January 14, 1958, page 3.

that 85 per cent of the traffic on highways leading into Tulsa were headed downtown" and the federal government allocated money "to relieve traffic congestion" in the city. In response, Tulsa's urban planners "visualized an expressway paralleling the Frisco railroad tracks" despite "opposition" from the local community. In order to spare downtown, Tulsa's planners and engineers "designed a loop around the business district with expressways running" around the downtown and then continuing their course outward (north, south, east, west) "like spokes on a wheel."[151]

This downtown-sparing loop project, however, called for the destruction of the Greenwood Avenue neighborhood, the site of Tulsa's historically famous African-American section "Black Wall Street" that had first been destroyed during the 1921 Race Riot. In 1967 the *Tulsa Tribune* ran a series of articles about the razing of the remaining buildings in the once-thriving area for the new raised-highway to loop around downtown that provides a good idea of the ambivalence of center-city Tulsans to the development project. After the completion of the "30-foot above ground" expressway in Greenwood, the remaining business-district stretch at the intersection of Greenwood and Archer would "be a lonely, forgotten lane ducking under the shadows of a big overpass" and "every forecast is that some urban renewal project will push down the buildings that have not already been torn down by the wrecking crews clearing right of way for the superhighway."[152] These businesses in the Greenwood-Archer district have managed to survive, and thrive, despite the gloomy tone of the *Tribune*'s article.

The most significant downtown development project was the creation of the Civic Center. The Civic Center circa 1960 covered "12 square blocks, counting the federal building and the two blocks for parking" in the area "between Third and Sixth Streets and Denver and Houston Avenues" in the western side of downtown. Work began on the Civic Center in 1952—over twenty years after renowned city planner Harland Bartholomew prepared a detailed plan for a six-square block Civic Center around the same area of Tulsa that failed to come to fruition due to the economic downturn of the Great Depression. The 1950s plan to build the Civic Center was largely based off

[151] "Looping Tulsa's New Loop," *Tulsa Tribune*, November 05, 1969.
[152] "An Old Tulsa Street is Slowly Dying," *Tulsa Tribune,* May 14, 1967.

Bartholomew's plan, with some adjustments to fit Tulsa's growth since Bartholomew submitted his plan in 1930.[153] A 1954 plan for the Civic Center, drawn by architect M. Murray McCune, presented the proposed Civic Center as an area with public buildings like the Courthouse, the City Hall, a Health Department Building, and also an Exposition Hall and landscaped surroundings. The plan did not come entirely to fruition, of course, but parts of the plan—including the Courthouse and the Exposition Hall--were built.[154] Over the next decade, the new Central Library, Municipal Building, and Federal Building, and an outdoor plaza were also completed in the Civic Center. By 1960, Tulsa was an automobile-based city, and also needed ample parking spaces. Many white-collar workers still commuted to work in downtown buildings, so building enough parking spaces downtown was a top priority for the City Planning Department. That year, Tulsa began its project to construct new "quarter-a-day" pay parking facilities around the Civic Center, as part of its plan to rejuvenate the entire area.[155] By 1974, the Civic Center's outdoor plaza was "a popular place" during the day where a "steady crowd" of downtown's white-collar workers "have lunch" on "comfortable benches and shady spots scattered around the fountain-splashed area."[156]

Postcard, c. 1965

Tulsa also experienced environmental problems as a direct result of its pro-development policy and economy centered on petroleum. The petroleum industry was the foundation of the economy for Tulsa, and the surrounding region, so Oklahoma's policymakers were reluctant to enact restrictive environmental regulatory measures. Tulsa, as the "Oil Capital of the World," is a city entirely built for automobiles, and based on the importance of oil and gas for the economy, but cleanliness has also been a goal.

[153] "Civic Center, a 35-Year Old Dream," *Tulsa Tribune*, July 26, 1965.
[154] "Civic Center Plan Offered," *Tulsa Tribune,* June 02, 1954.
[155] "Planners OK Civic Center Parking," *Tulsa Tribune,* February 15, 1960.
[156] "Plaza Becomes Popular Spot," *Tulsa Tribune,* July 06, 1974.

Tulsa's elite families, including many Oil Barons, wanted to be taken seriously for their high-culture, for their majestic mansions, and for the wealth they poured into projects beneficial to the municipality of Tulsa. The Philbrook and Gilcrease Museums—with core collections based on the mansion and art collections of local oilmen that were deeded to the City of Tulsa--are excellent examples of this. High-society and high-culture may be bought with petroleum money, but obvious pollution and sanitary problems take the gleam off the mansions, skyscrapers and elaborate Art Deco decorations. Tulsa's oil-money elite had good reason to want municipal ordinances implemented to improve sanitation.

A Private Garden, 1921

Sanitation was, therefore, important to the Tulsa municipality from the very beginning. Tulsa's first ordinances were passed from 1900 to 1905 (and published in 1905), before Tulsa was much of a city: Tulsa was referred to as a "second-class" municipality in the ordinances at that time. In these initial ordinances, Tulsa's sanitary code put the impetus on citizens to keep their residences clean. The town marshal was entrusted with enforcement of the code; the neighbors could complain to the marshal and he would decide what action (if any) to enforce. Residents were also expected to keep the street clear in front of their dwelling. The Board of Health was established in these 1900-1905 ordinances, and put in charge of managing waste such as it affected health, or seemed to pose a threat. This board was an attempt to address waste when it posed a public threat, and was not just a matter of disturbance such as was the town marshal's jurisdiction.[157] Tulsa's first City Charter was in 1908. This charter gave the city

[157] *Ordinances, "City of Tulsa," July 23, 1900 to April 10, 1905.* Xerox copy available at the Tulsa City-County Library.

government the explicit power to oversee and regulate garbage, especially once it posed a health threat or public disturbance.[158]

In 1917, Tulsa published amendments to its charter and new municipal ordinances. At this time, the municipality appointed "some person as the City Garbage Collector," whose duties were to "supply each of his garbage wagon drivers with a badge…" and it was unlawful for any other persons to collect the city's garbage. In turn, city residents were required to follow protocol in managing their rubbish bins (to preserve public cleanliness and well-kept appearance). Garbage was strictly defined: it was unlawful to throw away anything except "kitchen slop or kitchen garbage," and the garbage collector had authority to report noncompliant households to the Board of Health. Specifically, "paper, tin cans, broken glass or crockery ware, bottlers, old shoes, dead animals, dung, feculent matter" as well as other non-kitchen garbage were outlawed. These items were to be kept in separate containers and the disposal of such contents was to be carried out under the authority of the Board of Health, but was often done informally by the household which generated them because a special fee had to be paid to the City Trash Collector for disposal of this waste. The municipality also appointed a City Scavenger and "assistant employees" to aid the "proper disposal of garbage or night soil or other refuse matter," but with specific fees and regulations and only during daytime hours to prevent unauthorized scavenging by other persons. The Superintendent of Health was given the authority to investigate and charge households/persons who did not keep their premises clean, such as when garbage was strewn along their yard, and especially if these violations were noxious or obnoxious to neighbors or passer-by.[159]

---

[158] *Charter of the City of Tulsa, 1908.*

[159] *Complied Ordinances of the City of Tulsa, Oklahoma, 1917.*

Tulsa's rapid growth meant that by 1931 the City Charter required significant amendments and publication of revised city ordinances. These city ordinances have a more serious, scientific tone, befitting a large city. The municipality now had explicit power to "prevent any person from bringing, depositing or burying within the city limits, the carcasses of any dead animals, or other unwholesome substance, or matter, of filth of any kind, and to require prompt removal of the same, and impose all necessary penalties for the enforcement of the same." The City of Tulsa also claimed control of the five miles boundary around city limits to prevent unlawful dumping or health threats there. New standards for monitoring water quality of the Arkansas River, as well as regulations for preventing the spread of disease were also passed. The overall tone of this document shows Tulsa as a city with a strong sense of its identity and thus the need to regulate distasteful or unhealthful practices on public spaces.[160]

Electricity Plant, on the western bank of the Arkansas River

Over the following decades—up to the present day—Tulsa's revised City Charter and ordinances have continued the transition described above. The primary change since the 1960s and 1970s is toward meeting stricter national standards for sanitation and the environment. What is most illuminating about the City of Tulsa's sanitary standards is how similar they are to other cities in "developed" nations, like New York City, Toronto, and also Tel Aviv.[161] It is not hyperbole to say that city elites and policymakers saw proper sanitation as a defining feature of modern civilization.

[160] *Charter of the City of Tulsa 1908 with Amendments to 1931 and revised Ordinances of the City of Tulsa, 1931.*

[161] Benjamin Lawson, "Garbage Mountains: The Use, Redevelopment, and Artistic Representation of New York City's Fresh Kills, Greater Toronto's Keele Valley, and Tel Aviv's Hiriya Landfills," Dissertation: The University of Iowa, 2015.

Conclusion

From the beginning, the elites and policymakers of Tulsa and Tel Aviv sought to promote the modernity of their city. To do this, they defined their city as progressive, civilized, and boasting the latest industrial facilities and architectural trends. The process of modernization, however, had several significant detractions.

Tulsa Booster Train, 1905

The history of Tulsa and Tel Aviv, in particular, makes clear the problems of rapid modernization. The settlement of Tel Aviv and Tulsa relied on the false dichotomy of the "modern" as better than the "traditional," and hence these cities were based on an imperialistic ideology of Zionism and Manifest Destiny that claimed that the natives did not really matter because they were not civilized or modern. Tel Aviv and Tulsa also experienced huge sanitary problems, especially because these cities were proponents of rapid industrialization; in particular, Tulsa's life blood was the oil industry, which degraded the local environment significantly. Tel Aviv and Tulsa's settlers both (incorrectly) claimed a

Herzl Street, 1925

tabula rasa for their development, yet these cities' growth necessitated the destruction of existing nature, existing villages, and also homes and buildings—especially pre-1948 in neighborhoods like Manshiya at the border of Tel Aviv and Jaffa. Finally, Tulsa and Tel Aviv commissioned modernist-style architecture and the latest styles of urban planning to build a contemporary-looking city; because of this, building styles in Tulsa and Tel Aviv today are eclectic, based on the decade in which a specific building or area of the city was commissioned. Architecturally, the modernist style is just one style among many. The main problem with Tel Aviv and Tulsa's booster or founding myth is that these cities' elites believed the modern style of building cities was a panacea. They, simplistically, believed that their cities embodied the progress of civilization into the frontier.

Chapter Five

Experience

21st Century Tel Aviv and Tulsa

The city that exists today makes it very difficult to remember what was there before, and to imagine what would be there now in an alternative/parallel history if things had been different. The elites and elected officials of Tulsa and Tel Aviv presented a carefully constructed official image of their city. The means and methods of promotion were diverse, and included: press releases, photographs, and specially commissioned books. Actually building, and promoting, the city was the surest means of ensuring positive views of the city and emphasizing the discourse of the triumphal building of civilization in the frontier.

Walking around Tulsa versus Tel Aviv is a very different experience. Tulsa, like many North American cities, was built around the automobile and its sprawling development is based primarily on neighborhoods of single-family homes bordered every square mile by busy commercial boulevards. Tel Aviv, on the other hand, is mostly made up of densely packed multi-family residential buildings, with busy mixed-use commercial streets, and fits more with a European-style of planning. You could say that Tel Aviv feels older and larger than Tulsa, because Tel Aviv's development density is higher than Tulsa's.

Architecture is often privately commissioned and owned, but is a reflection of a city's identity and image—the patterns of development, including architecture, are the face it presents to the world at large. Tel Aviv's "Bauhaus" and Tulsa's "Art Deco" showed the world-at-large that these cities were modern and extremely wealthy. In Tulsa the architectural style took on more of a North American development pattern, with more emphasis on skyscrapers. In Tel Aviv the major style was International Style or Bauhaus, such as was the prevailing fashion in early-twentieth-century Europe. Tulsa had more "undeveloped land" around its borders, so it was able to grow, spread outward, with few geographic barriers except the Arkansas River. Tel Aviv had geographical boundaries like the Mediterranean Sea and Jaffa, and also preexisting settlements that blocked its sprawl somewhat; however, its suburbs are now huge. Tel Aviv's "suburbs" like Ramat Gan, Bat Yam, and Bnei Brak (to name a few) are very much like cities in their own right, and essentially mark the continuation of Tel Aviv; these "suburbs" have skyscrapers and dense development. Tulsa's "suburbs" or surrounding cities like Broken Arrow, Sand Springs, Owasso, and Jenks (to name a few) also blend into Tulsa's sprawl, but they seem less "urban" and are far smaller in population than Tel Aviv's neighbors.

Tel Aviv and Tulsa are not necessarily the same, but they do represent manifestations of the modern-style city. The argument of the preceding chapters was that Tulsa and Tel Aviv are similar in that they both developed quickly and their leaders and elite residents self-consciously promoted the city as modern in style. The establishment of cities with westernized land-development patterns was the means of normalizing European and American takeover of land. Today, without irony, people can refer to Tulsa as the "Most American of American Cities" and Tel Aviv as the flagship Israeli (Zionist) city. This chapter tells the story through reflections on specific parts of the city; photographs will form the basis of the narrative. The main theme is that the contemporary cities of Tulsa and Tel Aviv effectively cover up most traces of what was there before the cities were settled.

Experiencing contemporary Tulsa and Tel Aviv is the best way to make clear that the past is gone, or erased, with few traces. Many of the remaining traces are now tourist spots or museum sites. Some natural, physical-geographic, features like the Mediterranean seacoast and the Arkansas River remain, but most of the "natural environment" has also been erased.

Tulsa

The Council Oak

The Council Oak—which marks the location of the Lochapokas' original settlement in 1836—is located just to the south of downtown Tulsa, at 18th and Cheyenne streets. Today, the Council Oak stands in the shadow of a high-rise apartment building.

Downtown Tulsa—the area covered for most of this book--is the most "urban" of the city's regions, and includes a sizeable portion of the city's historically significant architecture from the early twentieth century. Other parts of Tulsa have significant newer buildings, but no part rivals downtown as a living museum of architectural fashions; indeed, few cities anywhere in the world have as many significant buildings from the 1920s and early 1930s grouped together in a single area. Tulsa is unique among U.S. cities simply because few buildings were there beforehand and the city's wealth was boundless during its initial decades due to the oil-money boom.

Tulsa's southern edge of downtown

Many of Tulsa's oldest and exquisitely decorated churches are in the southern part of downtown. Holy Family Cathedral (Catholic), Boston Avenue Methodist, and the

Christian Science church are notable examples; Trinity (Episcopal) and First Methodist church are in central downtown, but are also beautiful old churches worthy of mention.

The downtown of Tulsa is located by the curve of the Arkansas River, as it bends toward the southeast as it continues its course down to the Three Forks region of Muskogee.

Christian Science Church

Boston Avenue Methodist Church

Holy Family Cathedral

Public Service of Oklahoma

Bank of America Center

The southern section of downtown is where the newer skyscrapers, such as the 28-story and 388-foot-tall 110 West 7th Building (1971) and the 32-story 412-foot-tall Bank of America Center (1967), and smaller downtown buildings like hotels, the Oklahoma State University Medical Center, and apartments are located. Some Art Deco buildings are also there such as the Public Service of Oklahoma Building (completed 1929) and the Boston Avenue Methodist Church.

110 West 7th Building

This area is more spread out than other parts of downtown, because there is a greater distance between buildings, and the skyscrapers are freestanding instead of packed in together. The visual result is that the tall buildings do not blend together as much and each separate building stands out more--so this area feels like the edge of downtown and not like the central city core.

BOK Center

In the western part of downtown is the Civic Center area, including the Cox Convention Center, federal building, courthouse, and the Central branch of the Tulsa City County Library. The recently completed (2008) BOK Center is Tulsa's major stadium and auditorium; it finally realized the original 1950s plan for the Civic Center's proposed venue.

East of the BOK Center leads toward Tulsa's historic downtown core, where the initial oil-money skyscrapers and hotels are located. The Mayo Hotel (1925), an early high-rise hotel that was briefly Oklahoma's tallest building, is one of the highlights; east of the Mayo Hotel on 5th Street is the McFarlin Building (1918), which has a distinctive Florentine (Renaissance Italian) architectural style.

Mayo Hotel

The heart of the 1920s's oil-money downtown is Boston Avenue from 3rd Street to 5th Street. Here is the Cosden Building (1918), which was one of Tulsa's early skyscrapers,

Cosden Building

and is now the base of the 36-story and 513-foot-tall Mid-Con Tower (1980s), which has a retro-style green-colored copper roof and decorations that mimic the Art Deco and neo-Gothic styles popular in early-twentieth-century skyscrapers. The 3200 Boston Building, formerly the First National Bank of Tulsa building, is still prominent, although no longer the tallest skyscraper as it was from 1928 to 1967. The Atlas Life Building

3200 Boston Building

(1922) is a distinctive 10-story early skyscraper that began as an office building but now serves as a hotel. The Philtower (1928), another oil-money art-deco skyscraper, is less tall but stands out from a distance due to its multi-colored steeple.

Mid-Con Tower

Philower

Atlas Life Building

Philcade

First Place Tower, and surroundings

Trinity Episcopal Church, looking north on Cincinnati Street

The main streets of downtown, such as Boston and Main and 4th and 5th, are enclosed by the concrete canyons of the skyscrapers, and have a feeling not out of place for larger cities like Chicago or Lower Manhattan; of note is the 41-story and 516-foot-tall First Place Tower (1973). Tulsa's downtown is, admittedly, smaller and only a few streets boast that atmosphere, but Tulsans have pride for their downtown skyline, even if over the last few decades the downtown has experienced decay and disuse.

Plaza at 3rd and Boston Streets

The Tulsa Vision 2000 and Vision 2025 redevelopment programs have had a positive influence on how Tulsa's downtown looks and feels, although it is still a work in progress. Urban lofts and apartments are being constructed and are becoming common in recent years, as Tulsa works to renovate its downtown so that it maintains vibrancy after 5:00pm. Tulsa's city planners believe that having people live downtown is the first, crucial step—and to all appearances they are succeeding.

At the northern edge of the historic downtown core is the 52-story and 667-foot-tall BOK Tower (1975), formerly known as One Williams Tower, which is Tulsa's tallest building. This area is the Williams campus, where office buildings like the 23-story and 296 foot tall Williams Center-Tower II (1982) separate Tulsa's major skyscraper-lined north-south downtown street—Boston Avenue—from the Frisco tracks and the northern side of the downtown core; the Williams campus virtually marks the northern edge of the financial and office-building portion of downtown.

BOK Tower, formerly One Williams Tower

First Street, Tulsa's initial major east-west street, runs parallel to the Frisco tracks—Tulsa's initial railroad line. Most of the historical buildings on First Street are gone, such as Jeff Archer's General Store, for example, and are marked only by historical plaques on the sidewalk. The former Tulsa Union Depot is located off 1st Street and Boston Street and alongside

Tulsa Union Depot, now the Jazz Hall of Fame

the Frisco tracks, and now serves as Tulsa's Jazz Hall of Fame. Boston Street is blocked between the BOK Tower and the Frisco tracks, but instead of the street there is a pedestrian bridge that crosses the tracks next to the Union Depot building.

Frisco Tracks and Tulsa Union Depot

Although the entire area north of the Frisco tracks is being redeveloped and transformed, the process is ongoing; some open areas still exist to the northeast of downtown. This area, between the central downtown and the new ONEOK Field and the Greenwood-Archer district, is still somewhat open. All indications are that this open area (pictured above) will soon disappear and be redeveloped like the areas adjacent to it such as the Blue Dome District and the Brady Arts District.

North of the Frisco Tracks

ONEOK Field

Looking north from inside Philbrook Downtown

Philbrook Downtown

The Brady Arts District, on the northern edge of downtown, is one of the success stories. Tulsa's initial Convention Center (completed in 1914) is now known as the Brady Theater, and remains in use for theatrical and musical shows. The area surrounding the Brady Theater was historically a warehouse district, literally on the other side of the tracks from the heart of downtown. Today, these streets house many galleries, as well as Philbrook Downtown—the modern/contemporary and Native American branch of the Philbrook Museum of Art—which opened in

Brady Theater,
formerly the Convention Center

June 2013 in an "early twentieth century industrial warehouse."[162] Also noteworthy is Cain's Ballroom, established in 1930 at the site of a former Art Deco-style car garage, which has been the centerpiece of Tulsa's rock music scene since reopening in 1977.

Blue Dome Building

To the southeast of the Brady Arts District is the recently redeveloped Blue Dome District, which is Tulsa's major bar and club entertainment district. Architecturally, the area has historical buildings from Tulsa's early years, including the Blue Dome building, which was a Gulf oil station in the 1920s.

On the other side of the Crosstown Expressway (I 244) is Greenwood and Archer, and the last-remaining buildings of the flourishing African American commercial district. Despite the construction of the "spaghetti" overpasses and exit ramps of where US 75 and I 244 meet, this area has remained strong and now connects the revamped Brady Arts District and the new ONEOK Field with the Greenwood Cultural Center and OSU-Tulsa, the Tulsa branch of Oklahoma State University.

---

[162] Press Releases, Philbrook. Accessed January 2017. https://philbrook.org/about/press-releases/museum-opens-philbrook-downtown-june-14th

Mabel B. Little Heritage House

Most of the historical black neighborhoods in Tulsa have been destroyed, or erased due to "urban renewal." One of the few remnants of Tulsa's flourishing 1910s and 1920s African American district is the Mabel B. Little Heritage House, located between Greenwood and Archer and OSU-Tulsa. The "very existence" of this home "demonstrates that the working class Black family was, in some instances, able to rise above the racial discrimination, to build a substantial home that would parallel its counterparts in the elite white neighborhoods."[163]

Vernon A.M.E. Church

Located just across the street is the Vernon African Methodist Episcopal Church; established in 1905, burned down during the 1921 Race Riot, and rebuilt in 1925, the church is a landmark. "In the 1930s, Greenwood was a busy, busy, busy place," with "more than 145 businesses up and down Greenwood Avenue." The Vernon A.M.E. Church flourished through the 1950s, when "membership grew to nearly 1,200 people."[164]

[163] The Mabel B. Little Heritage House, Greenwood Cultural Center. Accessed January 2017. http://www.greenwoodculturalcenter.com/mabel-b-little-heritage-house

[164] "Vernon A.M.E. is witness to persistence," Tulsa World, August 10, 1991.

East of downtown is the Pearl District, which includes the beautiful landscaping of Centennial Park, and also the Art Deco-style Fire Alarm Building, which was built in 1930.

Fire Alam Building

To the southeast of downtown is historical Route 66, along 11th Street from the east and continuing on Southwest Boulevard to the southwest. Route 66 is a major tourist attraction for Tulsa, with many Route-66-themed businesses and historical signs. The Warehouse Market (1930) is especially noteworthy for its distinctive Art-Deco design.

Centennial Park

Tulsa, historically, was a racially segregated city, and this is reflected clearly in its development patterns. The areas south of the downtown were the white areas, and these areas have most of the non-downtown historical sites that still remain. As mentioned, the Tulsa Race Riot of 1921 destroyed the Black Wall Street area, which was one of the most flourishing African American neighborhoods in the entire nation. That area, centered on Greenwood Street, was able to rebuild, but problems reemerged in the 1960s, especially with the construction of the Crosstown Expressway through the historical heart of Greenwood, and the isolation of the small business strip at Greenwood and Archer. Urban renewal, even recently, has erased much

Warehouse Market

Arkansas River, near 31st St, circa 2000

of Tulsa's historical African American districts, and so most of Tulsa's growth has spread to the south, and to the east (away from the oil refineries across the Arkansas River from downtown).

Riverside Drive, which follows the east bank of the Arkansas River all the way to the suburb of Jenks, is one of Tulsa's most beautiful drives, and the centerpiece of Tulsa's ongoing Riverfront Parks redevelopment project—specifically the construction of the Gathering Place park centered around the pedestrian bridge and donated land (formerly the site of a huge mansion that was demolished to make the park possible) near 31st Street. The trail system that runs parallel to the river connects with biking-running-walking trail systems that spread out across Tulsa, out all the way to the suburbs.

Riverside Drive, 31st St, circa 2000

Clock, Utica Square

Utica Square, at 21st and Utica Streets, was one of Tulsa's early shopping centers outside of downtown; it opened in 1952. Located in the shadow of St. John Hospital (established 1926), Utica Square primarily serves Tulsa's upscale patrons, and it is well-known for its decorations—fountains, clocks, statues, and seasonal decorations.

St. John seen from Utica Square

The area not far south of downtown, south of 21st street near Utica, Lewis, Peoria Streets, is Tulsa's Old Money area. Chief among the attractions is Woodward Park, and the Rose Garden. Attractive, expensive houses surround the park area, and these neighborhoods are in high demand. Woodward Park was created in 1929, and covers 45 acres; the Rose Garden was added in 1935 as part of the New Deal's Works Progress Administration (WPA) work in Tulsa.

21st Street

Woodward Park

Philbrook

This very exclusive area includes some of Tulsa's oil mansions, most famously Waite Phillips's mansion Philbrook (near 27th and Peoria), which since 1938 has been a city-owned Museum of Art. The core collection of Philbrook includes Renaissance Italian paintings, 19th Century European and American paintings, and American Indian pottery.

Philbrook

The mansion is also significant for its history. Waite Phillips's mansion is a wonderful example of Tulsa's elite striving for high-culture, for sophistication, and for recognition that Oklahoma oilmen were "Renaissance Men" in their own right.

11th Street, the historical Route 66

Golden Driller, at the former IPE grounds

The area between Old Money and the downtown is more modest, yet still significant. 15th street, Cherry Street, is one attraction. This area has become popular for restaurants, cafes, and entertainment. Much of this area is residential, except for the major streets (11th, 15th).

The University of Tulsa (TU) is at 11th and Harvard, along the historical Route 66, and the neighborhoods around this institution have recently been "gentrified" to a degree; old restaurants and bars and shops remain in the area.

South of TU is the Expo Center, and the historical site of the International Petroleum Exposition (IPE) grounds, where the 75-foot-tall Golden Driller statue has stood since 1966.

Plaza near 61st and Yale

Tulsa's major streets on the north-south axis are named—such as Sheridan, Harvard,

Memorial—and the streets on the east-west axis are numbered. For residents of Tulsa, the combination of street names and numbers calls to mind the characteristics of specific neighborhoods, commercial districts, or institutions. Whether rich or poor, development in Tulsa follows a basic pattern: the major streets are commercially zoned and form a grid system every square mile, inside which residences are the primary feature.

Tulsa has sprawled outwardly instead of rebuilding already-occupied areas of town; old houses are typically sold and resold, instead of being demolished to make way for newer buildings. Therefore, with few exceptions, the newest homes in Tulsa are found at the outskirts of town and also in the surrounding suburbs. Moreover, when going to a specific neighborhood you will find homes mostly built at the same time and so whole sections of Tulsa are like time capsules of a certain decade; for example, the neighborhoods around Edison High School (1956) circa 41st Street between Harvard and Lewis, are from the 1950s, and were virtual suburbs at the time they were built. Today, these neighborhoods have kept value well, and the land is desirable, so a few homeowners are only recently beginning to construct larger, newer homes in this area, but that is still relatively uncommon.

High-rises along I44, near 41st St.

The intersection of I44 and the Broken Arrow Expressway, by 41st and Sheridan, hosts many office buildings, hotels, colleges, and commercial venues; the meeting place of these two highways has created a sort of mini downtown, constructed in the 1960s in direct competition with Tulsa's historical center. The Promenade Mall (1965), one of Tulsa's indoor mall attractions of the 1960s, is also nearby. This mall, today, struggles somewhat to compete with the newer and larger Woodland Hills Mall at 71st and Memorial, which is now Tulsa's primary commercial district.

Further south, along the Arkansas River, is Tulsa's second-tallest skyscraper: the sixty-story and 648-foot tall City Plex Tower. The City Plex complex was originally built (1979-1981) by an influential Christian, Oral Roberts, to serve as a hospital--the complex's original name was the City of Faith. Roberts's hospital plan quickly failed and the towers have since been converted to office space. In contrast to the City of Faith's failure, Oral Roberts University (established 1965), located nearby, has been very successful; its campus architecture is best described as "1960s futuristic" in style.

City Plex Towers

Tulsa International Airport

Tulsa's International Airport and aerospace industries and the Spartan School of Aeronautics are located in the far northeast section of the city, along the Gilcrease Expressway (US 11) and near I 244. This area, when selected for the airport in the late-1920s, was well outside of city limits, and today the airport marks the virtual barrier between Tulsa and the suburb of Owasso.

Spartan Aeronautics

Most of Tulsa's factories are located in the northern side of the city, near the airport as well as along the major east-west streets that lead into the city toward downtown, such as Pine Street. The far north of Tulsa, along streets like Apache (the main street north of Pine) and Pine feels a bit like a smaller town, in that older neighborhoods are spread out and co-exist with empty fields (including dump sites and formerly industrial areas) and the commercial venues are fewer and farther between than in most parts of Tulsa. The big Tulsa Community College (TCC) North Campus, located at the intersection of Apache and Harvard Streets, is a draw for development, as many commercial venues--such as the Tulsa-based QuikTrip gas station and convenience store—have opened up locations there.

A factory on Pine St.

Heading back to the west, Southwest Boulevard—the historical Route 66—crosses the Arkansas River on the 11th St. bridge in the south of downtown, and then branches south-west past the petroleum tanks and refineries.

Old Route 66, Southwest Boulevard

Past downtown, still to the north of the Arkansas River, is a residential area that flanks the huge oil refineries and petroleum tanks that take up most of the southern side of the Arkansas River at the bend in the river near to downtown Tulsa. The neighborhoods in this West Tulsa area are predominately working class, and quite often the smell of the refineries is in the air.

Oil Tanks, on Southwest Boulevard

Some of the oilmen chose to live outside the city, preferring the countryside. To the north of this neighborhood area is the Gilcrease Hills, the area of Gilcrease Museum and the former home of oilman Thomas Gilcrease.

A visitor to Tulsa would be forgiven for not noticing much of the city's pre-American-settlement past: there is simply not much left to see, because the urban development has covered up nearly all traces.

Tel Aviv

Tel Aviv is oriented primarily along a north-south axis alongside the Mediterranean Sea. The areas in the south, including Jaffa, are older and the areas to the north are much newer. Income levels in the north are generally higher than in the south (although Old City Jaffa is becoming a hot spot for millionaires). Much of the city proper of Tel Aviv—as is the case for Tulsa—blends seamlessly with the neighboring cities and suburbs. Tel Aviv's metropolitan area is roughly three-times bigger than Tulsa's, so there is a difference in scale; again, my argument is not that Tulsa and Tel Aviv are the same, but that they exhibit similar features, especially in terms of rapid settlement, booster promotion of modernity, and the erasure of pre-settlement history. Walking or driving around either Tel Aviv or Tulsa, the visitor will see only the urbanscape and land-development patterns that let on very little about these cities' complex histories.

Central Tel Aviv

Old City Jaffa

In Tel Aviv, the pre-Zionist past is visible most clearly in Old City Jaffa, which is a curious relic, cleared out and stripped of its Arab character; to critics, Jaffa today is only a shell, and it is merely an ahistorical tourist attraction (because the real history has been ruthlessly sanitized). Regardless, it is clear that the architectural styles in Old City Jaffa are in stark contrast to the modernist-style buildings, houses and businesses, and skyscrapers that cover most areas of Tel Aviv.

St. Peter's Church, Old City Jaffa

Gentrification in Jaffa

Tel Aviv's ahistorical founding myth is that it began as a city built on the empty sands, and it is still very difficult to find simple traces of the pre-Zionist past.

New Mansions near Old City Jaffa

Tools like urban renewal and constructing luxury hotels and apartments, and simply replacing signs to fit Israel's use of the Hebrew language, are the means by which Tel Aviv has virtually erased Jaffa, and pre-Israel Palestinian Arab settlements, from the map.

Old City Jaffa

Old City Jaffa is, today, a pleasant area, but a strangely lifeless place. Parts of the Old City's walls still remain, but few of the buildings inside those walls remain, and the formerly center-city area is mostly green lawn and landscaping. Signs have been strategically posted to inform visitors what cleared-out areas used to be like; for example, a sign pointing out where Jaffa's small Jewish community lived. Once (in 2014), as I was walking through Old City Jaffa, I heard a man (who was either a tour guide or a real estate salesman) telling his companions that demand for Jaffa's real estate was booming, because it was "like Jerusalem" because of its small, narrow passageways and ancient rock and romantic charm.

Jonah and the Whale statue, Old City Jaffa

House of Simon the Tanner, Old City Jaffa

Jaffa, seen from Jaffa Port

Today's hollow center of Old City Jaffa

From the high land inside Jaffa's walls, one may see Tel Aviv's skyline stretching all along the coast. The land area around Old City Jaffa rises well above the surrounding area, and so the Old City area offers lovely views. Most of Old City Jaffa was destroyed during violence outbreaks (e.g. the 1936 violence during which the British bombed Jaffa in retaliation) and war (e.g. 1948 War of Independence and its aftermath). Archeological digs are also ongoing at the site. Jaffa's tel has a much deeper history than the surface lets on.

View of Tel Aviv from Old City Jaffa

Jaffa is an ancient seaport, mentioned in the *Torah* or the *Old Testament* as the port where Jonah departed before he was swallowed by the whale. The Greek myth of Perseus and Andromeda also took place at Jaffa, as the rocks outside Jaffa Port are the rocks where Andromeda was chained as sacrifice to the Kraken. Jaffa is a famous destination for Christians, because St. Paul was staying there when he had the vision that led him to expand his teaching to the Gentiles (at the House of Simon the Tanner). Tourist buses roll up to the Old City plaza where visitors see the buildings like St. Peter's Church (1894) and may go to art galleries and boutiques. Inside the passageways of the walls are some residences, which have been gentrified and are very expensive.

Jaffa Port

Jaffa Port has recently been redeveloped, and a huge pavilion with shops and restaurants is there to serve tourists. The port itself is still in use, although only for small craft, as the rocks outside the port prevent any larger ships; in the past, large ships would anchor off shore and visitors would reach Jaffa by means of small landing boats.

The area around Jaffa is in the process of being gentrified. To the east of the Old City are the streets of Jaffa, notably the area of the Jaffa Flea Market—an open air market—and many shops and restaurants for tourists. The Clock Tower marks the entranceway to this district, but it is difficult to reach due to the heavy traffic. Many older neighborhoods surround the Jaffa city center, but not far to the south of the Old City is the recently constructed Andromeda Hill neighborhood of mansions for millionaires who desire a seafront view and easy access to the Old Town.

Jaffa Clock Tower

Jaffa, seen from the north

The Manshiya area, at the northernmost edge of Jaffa, is mostly gone. Hassan Bek mosque remains, as does the foundation of an old Palestinian house that is now part of the Etzl Museum (the Etzl was a Jewish military organization). Charles Clore Park is an expansive green space that geographically divides Jaffa from Tel Aviv.

Etzl Museum

Hassan Bek Mosque seen from Charles Clore Park

The buildings in the Neve Tzedek area, bordering on what used to be Manshiya, are very different in style than that typical of (post-1930) Tel Aviv; the buildings here are smaller, and built in the Mediterranean style of red-tile roofs. The streets here wind through the older neighborhoods, and do not conform to the straight and wide format of more-recent Tel Aviv. Probably because of the "quaint" or old-fashioned feel of these winding streets and old-fashioned houses in these older Jewish neighborhoods, this area is being redeveloped into a hotspot for art galleries and boutiques. Across Europe and North America, people are beginning to seek out older areas as being "arty" and Israel is following that trend. Skyscrapers near the neighborhood are highly visible landmarks.

Neve Tzedek

Neve Tzedek

The White City

The heart of Tel Aviv is near the intersection of Allenby Street or Herzl Street with Rothschild Boulevard, located near the junction where the older, windier streets of the southern neighborhoods abruptly end and are replaced by the straight and wide streets of the White City. The White City refers to the many 1930s-1950s high-modernist buildings (referred to as either the Bauhaus Style or the International Style) that emphasize geometrical forms and have distinctive balconies. This architectural style emphasized the importance of function, and so the buildings were designed as "machines for living" (to quote Le Corbusier). The historically significant Herzliya Gymnasium (on the northern edge of Herzl Street) is long gone--demolished in the 1960s-- and the Shalom Meir Tower stands in its place.

Beit Ha'ir, Tel Aviv's first City Hall

Tel Aviv's original City Hall, Beit Ha'ir (בית העיר), is now a museum of the city's history. Located in central Tel Aviv, Beit Ha'ir is a classic example of the refinements possible in a high-modernist public building.

Mayor's Office, Beit Ha'ir

One of the highlights is the office of Meir Dizengoff—Tel Aviv's first mayor.

From Beit Ha'ir's balcony—an essential feature of Tel Aviv's White City style--you may see pleasing views of the central city.

View from the rooftop balcony, Beit Ha'ir

View of Bialik St. from the Mayor's Office, Beit Ha'ir

Most of central Tel Aviv is well kept up and tourist friendly, but throughout the central sections of the city (as well as the southern sections) there are many buildings in need of, or in the process of, remodeling; graffiti is also extremely common across the city.

Vacant building with grafitti, central Tel Aviv

One of the top destinations in central Tel Aviv is the Carmel Market, an open-air market that specializes in fresh fruits and vegetables and spices.

Carmel Market

Rothschild Boulevard

Rothschild Boulevard remains the center of the city today. It is a divided boulevard, with park space between the lanes, and the houses that line the boulevard are many of the city's finest. Rothschild Boulevard begins on its western side at Herzl Street, and it does not connect to the sea or pass through the older neighborhoods like Neve Tzedek. At the eastern edge of Rothschild Boulevard are attractions such as the Culture Palace (home of the Israel Philharmonic Orchestra) and the Helena Rubenstein Pavilion of the Tel Aviv Museum of Art.

Skyscrapers in Central Tel Aviv

Skyscrapers were not historically common in Tel Aviv, but in recent decades towering office buildings, hotels, and luxury apartments have sprung up along the coastline, along the core of Rothschild Boulevard, and especially along the Ayalon Expressway that marks Tel Aviv's eastern boundary.

Skyscrapers along the Ayalon Expressway, seen from nothern Tel Aviv

Tel Aviv has several important north-south streets. Hayarkon Street parallels the coastline, and is full of hotels. Ben Yehuda Street roughly parallels Hayarkon a block inland, and is a major thoroughfare with shops, restaurants and hotels; Ben Yehuda merges into Allenby Street, which boasts many of the early Bauhaus-style buildings. Dizengoff Street has been

Hayarkon Street

City Hall, Rabin Square

compared to Paris's Champs Elysees, for its many fashion shops, cafes and restaurants; Dizengoff Center (1977) is one of Tel Aviv's major malls; Dizengoff Square is one of Tel Aviv's famous urban parks. Ibn Gabirol Street is roughly the east-west dividing street (i.e., in the center of the city) and is more contemporary in architectural style (1950s-recent) and is the location of Rabin Square—a common place for political demonstrations—next to the new City Hall building (1966), a wonderful example of 1960s Brutalist Style architecture.

Tel Aviv Museum of Art

The areas east of Ibn Gabirol Street are newer, and typically urban. One of the major destinations is the Tel Aviv Museum of Art, which has a distinctive new avant-garde wing and a large plaza (shared with the Public Library).

Houses in North Tel Aviv

Dizengoff Street

Hotels along the beaches

Tel Aviv Marina

The neighborhoods in northern Tel Aviv are more residential, and the houses there mimic the style of the White City but in simplistic ways—for example, they have faux balconies instead of the real thing.

Plaza by the Museum of Art

These city streets are still pleasant, perhaps cleaner than the streets of southern Tel Aviv, but seem to lack the historical veneer. The north is, however, home to many beaches and hotels that serve tourists visiting for beach vacations. Moreover, the highly-successful Hayarkon Park surrounds the Yarkon River—historically Tel Aviv's northern boundary—and there are many jogging and biking trails. Tel Aviv University is located not far north of the Yarkon River, in the neighborhood of Ramat Aviv.

Hayarkon Park at sunset

Bridge over the Yarkon River

Tel Aviv Port, Reading D Plant in background

Boardwalk, near Tel Aviv Port

Tel Aviv Port is probably the major entertainment venue in northern Tel Aviv. Derelict for many years, Tel Aviv Port has recently been redeveloped into a boardwalk, club scene, and shopping and dining area; remnants and artifacts of old Tel Aviv Port—such as the crane—are still on display although the port is no longer in use.

Hiriya (top left) seen from Ben-Gurion International Airport

A small, national, airport is located just north of the Yarkon River from Tel Aviv Port, but the significant airport is the Ben-Gurion International Airport located about 20 miles to the east of Tel Aviv, at the edge of the Tel Aviv metropolitan region. The Ben-Gurion Airport (est. 1936, as Wilhelma Airport) is the primary port of entry to Israel, and it serves Jerusalem as well but the airport is virtually (but not officially) located in Tel Aviv.

Tel Aviv's major garbage landfill, the Hiriya landfill (1952-1998), is located not far to the west of Ben-Gurion International Airport, and today it is being redeveloped into a huge (2000+ acres) public park: Ariel Sharon Park. The landfill was established in 1952 at the former site of a Palestinian village: Al Khayriyya. Although this sounds bad—to build a garbage dump on the site of a former village—this is extremely common in Israel. Before 1948, Palestinian-Arab villages covered much of the land in today's Tel Aviv metropolitan region. In Israel, it is a truism that these villages used to be in the locations now covered by Israeli cities and towns, farms and industries. The Hiriya landfill is just an especially clear example.

Conclusion

The success of a city has much to do with promotion, in order to attract investors, new residents, and companies. Tulsa and Tel Aviv were masters of this process. Because of this success, the elites, boosters, and policymakers of cities are constantly planning and manipulating the image of their city. This is reflected in development projects (e.g., parks, highways, public buildings, museums, monuments) and in ideological projects (e.g., exhibitions, books), as well as in deciding which aspects of history are excluded from the image. Decades of this sort of image-promotion in Tulsa and Tel Aviv has made it extremely difficult for residents and visitors in Tel Aviv and Tulsa to find traces in the city of what the area was like before Euro-American settlement.

We often take human-constructed environments for granted today, but doing so blinds us to the very real alternatives that existed. Cities like Tulsa and Tel Aviv make a good starting point for reconsidering the basis of modern-style city building, because they are so young (roughly 125 years old), so brash, and ultimately fascinating. Reading the history of Tulsa and Tel Aviv gives the impression that success was never easy or inevitable, so the city boosters fervently promoted the rationale of bringing modern civilization to the frontier and kept up the hopeful talk until it became real; now that the cities exist in their present form it is difficult to imagine the "frontier" of their boosters' imagination. Today, Tel Aviv and Tulsa are still true to type: they have erased most traces of the past and remain focused on the future.

List of Images

Front Cover

"Jaffa: The Bay." PikiWiki Israel 41469 Tel Aviv. Source: Pikiwiki, Public Domain. https://commons.wikimedia.org/wiki/File:PikiWiki_Israel_41469_Tel_Aviv.jpg

Tulsa's skyline (detail). From the top right side of "The Smithsonian Institution Hall of Petroleum Mural," 13'x56', 1966. Source: on display at the Tulsa International Airport; photo by Benjamin A. Lawson, all rights reserved.

Opening pages

Jaffa Environs, 1912. Source: University of Texas Maps Digital Collection, From *Palestine and Syria Handbook for Travellers* by Karl Baedeker, 5th Edition, 1912. https://www.lib.utexas.edu/maps/historical/jaffa_1912.jpg

Tel Aviv Plan, 1925. Source: Public Domain, https://commons.wikimedia.org/wiki/File:Geddes_Plan_for_Tel_Aviv_1925.jpg

Tel Aviv Map, north, 1950s. Tel Aviv-Yafo No. 1, 1:10,000, Edition 2-AMS, Series K931. U.S. Army Map Service, 1958. Source: University of Texas Maps Digital Collection. http://www.lib.utexas.edu/maps/world_cities/txu-oclc-60496256-tel_aviv_yafo1-1958.jpg

Tel Aviv Map, south, 1950s. Tel Aviv-Yafo No. 2, 1:10,000, Edition 2-AMS, Series K931. U.S. Army Map Service, 1958. Source: University of Texas Maps Digital Collection.. http://www.lib.utexas.edu/maps/world_cities/txu-oclc-60496256-tel_aviv_yafo2-1958.jpg

Creek Lands (Tulsa is in the top right), 1890s. Map showing progress of allotment in Creek Nation. From *Commission to the Five Civilized Tribes,* Dana, C. H. 1899. Source: Library of Congress.. https://www.loc.gov/item/2007627492/

Tulsa Map, 1920s. "Enumeration District Maps for the Twelfth through the Sixteenth Censuses of the United States, 1900-1940." Images. FamilySearch. http://FamilySearch.org : accessed 2016. Citing NARA microfilm publication A3378. National Archives and Records Administration, Washington D.C. Image 796. Source: Tulsa City-County Library, Digital Collection. http://cdm15020.contentdm.oclc.org/cdm/singleitem/collection/p16063coll3/id/234

Tulsa County Map, 1940s. "Enumeration District Maps for the Twelfth through the Sixteenth Censuses of the United States, 1900-1940" part 4. Images. FamilySearch. http://FamilySearch.org : accessed 2016. Citing NARA microfilm publication A3378. National Archives and Records Administration, Washington D.C. Images 763-766. Source: Tulsa City-County Library, Digital Collection. http://cdm15020.contentdm.oclc.org/cdm/compoundobject/collection/p16063coll3/id/196/rec/1

Tulsa Map, 1960s. American Automobile Association map. Source: Courtesy of Linda Lawson.

Chapter 1

Tulsa Booster Party, 1908. "Tulsa Pioneer Boosters at the War, Navy and State Building, Washington, D.C." Source: Public Domain; Clarence Douglas, *The History of Tulsa* (Chicago: S.J. Clark Publishing Company, 1921), 195.

The Founding of Tel Aviv: Ahuzat Bayit, 1909. Source: Public Domain, https://commons.wikimedia.org/wiki/Category:Historical_images_of_Tel_Aviv-Yafo#/media/File:TelAviv-Founding.jpg.

Jaffa, 19th Century. "From the sea, Jaffa, Holy Land, (i.e. Israel]," c. 1890. From Detroit Publishing Co., catalogue J foreign section (Detroit, MI: Detroit Photographic Company, 1905). Source: Library of Congress. http://www.loc.gov/pictures/item/2002724990/

Herzl Street and the Gymnasium, 1920s. Source: Public Domain, via Pikiwiki, https://commons.wikimedia.org/wiki/File:PikiWiki_Israel_41426_Tel_Aviv.jpg

Tulsa, 1910. "Tulsa, Okla. from corner [of] Second and Boston Streets," photo by Clarence Jack, c. 1910. Source: Library of Congress. https://www.loc.gov/item/2007662699/

Boston Avenue Methodist Church. Source: Public Domain, https://upload.wikimedia.org/wikipedia/commons/e/e8/Boston_Avenue_Methodist_Church_South%2C_Tulsa%2C_Okla_%2862996%29.jpg

Tel Aviv postcard. Source: Public Domain, via Pikiwiki, https://commons.wikimedia.org/wiki/Category:Historical_images_of_Tel_Aviv-Yafo#/media/File:PikiWiki_Israel_41461_Tel_Aviv.jpg

Tulsa at Night. Source: Digital Prairie, Oklahoma Department of Libraries. http://digitalprairie.ok.gov/cdm/compoundobject/collection/okpostcards/id/1181/rec/10

Rothschild Boulevard, 1930s. Source: Public Domain, via Pikiwiki, https://commons.wikimedia.org/wiki/Category:Historical_images_of_Tel_Aviv-Yafo#/media/File:PikiWiki_Israel_45651_Rotshild_Boulevard.jpg

Tulsa's Rose Garden at Woodward Park, Source: Digital Prairie, Oklahoma Department of Libraries.
http://digitalprairie.ok.gov/cdm/compoundobject/collection/okpostcards/id/1718/rec/15

Tel Aviv's Modernist Style Buildings. Source: Photo by Benjamin Lawson, all rights reserved.

Tulsa's Modernist Style Buildings. Source: Photo by Benjamin Lawson, all rights reserved.

Native American Statue, Philbrook. Source: Photo by Benjamin Lawson, all rights reserved.

Independence Park, north-western Tel Aviv. Source: Photo by Benjamin Lawson, all rights reserved.

Chapter 2

Council Oak. Source: Photo by Benjamin Lawson, all rights reserved.

Fort Gibson. Source: Photo by Benjamin Lawson, all rights reserved.

Railroads in Indian Territory. "Indian Territory showing railroad systems, June 30, 1902." Department of the Interior and United States Commission to the Five Civilized Tribes, 1902. Source: Library of Congress. https://www.loc.gov/item/2007627490/

Tulsa, 1894. Early Street Scene, 1894, Source: Clarence Douglas, *The History of Tulsa,* 1921 (Public Domain), page 163.

Frisco RR Bridge and Wagon Bridge over the Arkansas River, 1909. Source: Digital Prairie, Oklahoma Department of Libraries.
http://digitalprairie.ok.gov/cdm/compoundobject/collection/okpostcards/id/1850/rec/3

Bird's-Eye View of Tulsa, 1918. Fowler & Kelly. Pasaic [sic] N.J. [1918]. Source: Library of Congress https://www.loc.gov/resource/g4024t.pm007160/

Cosden Refinery, Source: Clarence Douglas, *The History of Tulsa,* 1921 (Public Domain), page 211.

Tulsa Race Riot, 1921. Smoke billowing over Tulsa, Oklahoma during 1921 race riots, Alvin C. Krupnick Co., c. 1921. Source: Library of Congress. https://www.loc.gov/item/95517018/

Aftermath of the Race Riot. Smoldering ruins of African American's homes following race riots in Tulsa, Okla., in 1921, Alvin C. Krupnick Co., c. 1921. Source: Library of Congress. https://www.loc.gov/item/95517072/

Oil Field near Tulsa c. 1921. Source: Clarence Douglas, *The History of Tulsa,* (Pubic Domain) 1921, page 207.

Tulsa Mansions, 1921. Source: Clarence Douglas, *The History of Tulsa,* (Pubic Domain) 1921, pages 625-6.

First National Bank of Tulsa Building. Source: Digital Prairie, Oklahoma Department of Libraries. http://digitalprairie.ok.gov/cdm/compoundobject/collection/okpostcards/id/1715/rec/4

Visit Oklahoma! 1952. *Visit Oklahoma: Travel Stamp Album and Guide Book* (Oklahoma City, OK: Oklahoma Planning and Resources Board, 1952). Source: Courtesy of Linda Lawson.

Central Tulsa, c. 2000. Source: Photo by Benjamin Lawson, all rights reserved.

Jaffa's Orchards. "From the garden, Jaffa, Holy Land, (i.e. Israel)," c. 1890. From Detroit Publishing Co., catalogue J foreign section (Detroit, MI: Detroit Photographic Company, 1905). Source: Library of Congress. http://www.loc.gov/pictures/item/2002724991/

Members of Ahuzat Bayit, 1909. Source: Public Domain, https://commons.wikimedia.org/wiki/File:Ahuzan_Baiyt22.jpg

Allenby Street, 1930s. "Ramleh Tel-Aviv. Allenby Square." American Colony (Jerusalem). Photo Dept., 1934-39. Source: Library of Congress. http://www.loc.gov/pictures/item/mpc2004003004/PP/

Jaffa Port, 1930s. "Palestine disturbances 1936. Numerous Jaffa lighters safe behind the new break-water in the lighter port, showing the long arm[?] of concrete in distance reaching out to Andromeda's Rocks." American Colony (Jerusalem). Photo Dept., 1936. Source: Library of Congress. https://www.loc.gov/item/mpc2010003740/PP/

Palestinian Villages, c. 1948. "Palestine," by Sami Hadawi, Palestine Arab Refugee Office [S.l., 1949]. Source: Library of Congress. https://www.loc.gov/item/98687122/

Manshiya in Ruins, 1948. "Manshiya in 1948," Beit Gidi Etzl Museum Exhibits, no author listed. Source: Public Domain, https://commons.wikimedia.org/wiki/File:Manshiya_IMG_0850.JPG

Dolphinarum's ruins, 2014. Source: Photo by Benjamin Lawson, all rights reserved.

Central Tel Aviv, 2014. Source: Photo by Benjamin Lawson, all rights reserved.

Hotels seen from Charles Clore Park. Source: Photo by Benjamin Lawson, all rights reserved.

Chapter 3

Palestine, 1776. Charte worauf das Lüdischeland: nach den alten Völckern und XII Stämen Israels vorgesstellet wird nach dem entwurff des Herrn W.A. Bachiene. I. E. Vetter, [Maastricht] : W.A. Bachiene, 1776. Source: Library of Congress. https://www.loc.gov/item/2011585237/

French exploration in North America, c. 1680s. "Carte de la Louisiane ou des voyages du Sr. De La Salle." Jean Baptiste Louis Franquelin, [S.l, 1896-1901]. Source: Library of Congress. https://www.loc.gov/resource/g3300.ct000656/

Louisiana Territory, 1803. "Louisiana." From *Arrowsmith & Lewis New and Elegant General Atlas*, 1804. Samuel Lewis and Aaron Arrowsmith. Source: Library of Congress. https://www.loc.gov/item/2001620468/

American Progress. "Westward the course of destiny Westward ho! Manifest destiny." George A. Crofutt, c. 1873. Source: Library of Congress. https://www.loc.gov/item/97507547/

Turkish Palestine. From *Palestine*, by Claude Reignier Conder. New York: Dodd, Mead and Co., 1887. Source: Project Guttenberg. http://www.gutenberg.org/files/43588/43588-h/43588-h.htm#map_VII

Indian Territory cigarette card, c. 1888. Major, Knapp & Co., printer, N.Y. : Major, Knapp & Co., Park Pl., N.Y., between 1885 and 1890. Source: Library of Congress. https://www.loc.gov/resource/ppmsca.39615/

Chapter 4

The Bazaar, Jaffa, 1896-1914. Jaffa (Joppa) and environs. The bazaar. American Colony, Jerusalem. Source: Library of Congress. https://www.loc.gov/item/mpc2004007027/PP/

Fishermen at Jaffa. Picture Postcard, by S. Narinsky. Jamal Brothers, no. 19, Jerusalem, Palestine, 1921 Source: Library of Congress. https://www.loc.gov/item/mamcol.043/

Buildings under construction, Tel Aviv 1930s. Source: Pikiwiki, Public Domain. https://commons.wikimedia.org/wiki/File:PikiWiki_Israel_40694_Tel_aviv.jpg

A Factory in Tel Aviv, c. 1925-1940. Tel Aviv industries. Taken either by the American Colony Photo Department or its successor, the Matson Photo Service. Source: Library of Congress. https://www.loc.gov/item/mpc2005007964/PP/

Tel Aviv Industries, c. 1925-1940. Taken either by the American Colony Photo Department or its successor, the Matson Photo Service. Source: Library of Congress. https://www.loc.gov/item/mpc2005007960/PP/

Tel Aviv Port, 1938. "Official opening of Tel Aviv Port. Lighter basin taken on opening day, showing sheds in dis[tance]." American Colony. Jerusalem. Source: Library of Congress. https://www.loc.gov/item/mpc2010002595/PP/

Buses and autos in Tel Aviv, c. 1930s. Taken either by the American Colony Photo Department or its successor the Matson Photo Service; created between 1920 and 1946. Source: Library of Congress. http://www.loc.gov/pictures/item/mpc2004000481/PP/

Tel Aviv bathing beach, 1940s. Matson Photo Service, c. 1940-46. Source: Library of Congress. https://www.loc.gov/item/mpc2005009096/PP/

Tulsa's Frisco Railroad. Tulsa's First Transcontinental Train Source: Clarence Douglas, *The History of Tulsa,* 1921 (Public Domain), page 171.

Streetcar in downtown, 1909 (detail). "Tulsa, Oklahoma" created by Clarence Jack. Source: Library of Congress. https://www.loc.gov/item/2007662700/

5th and Main, c. 1921. 5th and Main, looking north. Source: Clarence Douglas, *The History of Tulsa,* 1921 (Public Domain), page 183.

First Interstate Shipment of Freight by Airplane, Tulsa to Kansas City, August 14, 1919. Source: Clarence Douglas, *The History of Tulsa,* 1921 (Public Domain), page 589.

Gas Station converted into a Bar, Tulsa. Created by John Vachon, 1942. Source: Library of Congress. https://www.loc.gov/item/owi2001012103/PP/

Oil Cars on the Frisco Railroad, Tulsa. 1942. "Tulsa, Oklahoma. Oil tank cars in the Frisco railroad yards," Created by John Vachon, 1942. Source: Library of Congress. https://www.loc.gov/resource/fsa.8d09199/

Tulsa Postcard, c. 1965. Source: Courtesy of Linda Lawson.

Mural of Tulsa's Petroleum Origins, 1966. "The Smithsonian Institution Hall of Petroleum Mural," 13'x56', 1966. Source: on display at the Tulsa International Airport; photo by Benjamin A. Lawson, all rights reserved.

Postcard C. 1965. Source: Courtesy of Linda Lawson.

Electricity Plant on the western bank of the Arkansas River. Source: Photo by Benjamin Lawson, all rights reserved.

A Private Garden. Source: Public Domain; Clarence Douglas, *The History of Tulsa,* 1921 (Public Domain), 191.

Tulsa Booster Train, 1905. "Tulsa, I.T.—Delegation at Terre Haute, IND, March 16th 1905." Source: Public Domain; Clarence Douglas, The History of Tulsa, 1921 (Public Domain), 195.

Herzl Street, 1925. Source: Public Domain.
https://commons.wikimedia.org/wiki/File:Herzel_Street,_1925_-_detail_P1080436.JPG

Chapter 5

Council Oak. Source: Photo by Benjamin Lawson, all rights reserved.

Tulsa's southern edge of downtown. Source: Photo by Benjamin Lawson, all rights reserved.

Boston Avenue Methodist Church. Source: Photo by Benjamin Lawson, all rights reserved.

Holy Family Cathedral. Source: Photo by Benjamin Lawson, all rights reserved.

Christian Science Church. Source: Photo by Benjamin Lawson, all rights reserved.

Public Service of Oklahoma. Source: Photo by Benjamin Lawson, all rights reserved.

110 West 7th Building. Source: Photo by Benjamin Lawson, all rights reserved.

Bank of America Center. Source: Photo by Benjamin Lawson, all rights reserved.

BOK Center. Source: Photo by Benjamin Lawson, all rights reserved.

Cosden Building. Source: Photo by Benjamin Lawson, all rights reserved.

3200 Boston Building. Source: Photo by Benjamin Lawson, all rights reserved.

Mid-Con Tower. Source: Photo by Benjamin Lawson, all rights reserved.

Philtower. Source: Photo by Benjamin Lawson, all rights reserved.

Atlas Life Building. Source: Photo by Benjamin Lawson, all rights reserved.

First Place Tower and surroundings. Source: Photo by Benjamin Lawson, all rights reserved.

Philcade. Source: Photo by Benjamin Lawson, all rights reserved.

Trinity Episcopal Church, looking north on Cincinnati Street. Source: Photo by Benjamin Lawson, all rights reserved.

3rd and Boston Streets. Source: Photo by Benjamin Lawson, all rights reserved.

BOK Tower, formerly One Williams Tower. Source: Photo by Benjamin Lawson, all rights reserved.

Tulsa Union Depot, now the Jazz Hall of Fame. Source: Photo by Benjamin Lawson, all rights reserved.

Frisco Tracks and Tulsa Union Depot. Source: Photo by Benjamin Lawson, all rights reserved.

North of the Frisco Tracks. Source: Photo by Benjamin Lawson, all rights reserved.

ONEOK Field. Source: Photo by Benjamin Lawson, all rights reserved.

Looking north from inside Philbrook Downtown. Source: Photo by Benjamin Lawson, all rights reserved.

Philbrook Downtown. Source: Photo by Benjamin Lawson, all rights reserved.

Brady Theater, formerly the Convention Center. Source: Photo by Benjamin Lawson, all rights reserved.

Blue Dome Building. Source: Photo by Benjamin Lawson, all rights reserved.

Mabel B. Little Heritage House. Source: Photo by Benjamin Lawson, all rights reserved.

Vernon A.M.E. Church. Source: Photo by Benjamin Lawson, all rights reserved.

Fire Alarm Building. Source: Photo by Benjamin Lawson, all rights reserved.

Centennial Park. Source: Photo by Benjamin Lawson, all rights reserved.

Warehouse Market. Source: Photo by Benjamin Lawson, all rights reserved.

Riverside Drive, 31st St, circa 2000. Source: Photo by Benjamin Lawson, all rights reserved.

Riverside Drive, 31st St, circa 2000. Source: Photo by Benjamin Lawson, all rights reserved.

Clock, Utica Square. Source: Photo by Benjamin Lawson, all rights reserved.

St. John seen from Utica Square. Source: Photo by Benjamin Lawson, all rights reserved.

21st Street. Source: Photo by Benjamin Lawson, all rights reserved.

Woodward Park. Source: Photo by Benjamin Lawson, all rights reserved.

Philbrook. Source: Photo by Benjamin Lawson, all rights reserved.

Philbrook. Source: Photo by Benjamin Lawson, all rights reserved.

11th Street, the historical Route 66. Source: Photo by Benjamin Lawson, all rights reserved.

Golden Driller statue. Source: Photo by Benjamin Lawson, all rights reserved.

Plaza near 61st and Yale. Source: Photo by Benjamin Lawson, all rights reserved.

High-rises along I44, near 41st St. Source: Photo by Benjamin Lawson, all rights reserved.

City Plex Towers. Source: Photo by Benjamin Lawson, all rights reserved.

Tulsa International Airport. Source: Photo by Benjamin Lawson, all rights reserved.

Spartan Aeronautics. Source: Photo by Benjamin Lawson, all rights reserved.

Old Route 66, Southwest Boulevard. Source: Photo by Benjamin Lawson, all rights reserved.

Oil Tanks, on Southwest Boulevard. Source: Photo by Benjamin Lawson, all rights reserved.

Central Tel Aviv. Source: Photo by Benjamin Lawson, all rights reserved.

Old City Jaffa. Source: Photo by Benjamin Lawson, all rights reserved.

St. Peter's Church, Old City Jaffa. Source: Photo by Benjamin Lawson, all rights reserved.

Gentrification in Jaffa. Source: Photo by Benjamin Lawson, all rights reserved.

New Mansions in Jaffa. Source: Photo by Benjamin Lawson, all rights reserved.

Old City Jaffa. Source: Photo by Benjamin Lawson, all rights reserved.

Jonah and the Whale statue, Old City Jaffa. Source: Photo by Benjamin Lawson, all rights reserved.

House of Simon the Tanner, Old City Jaffa.

Jaffa, seen from Jaffa Port. Source: Photo by Benjamin Lawson, all rights reserved.

Today's hollow center of Old City Jaffa. Source: Photo by Benjamin Lawson, all rights reserved.

View of Tel Aviv from Old City Jaffa. Source: Photo by Benjamin Lawson, all rights reserved.

Jaffa Port. Source: Photo by Benjamin Lawson, all rights reserved.

Jaffa Clock Tower. Source: Photo by Benjamin Lawson, all rights reserved.

Jaffa, seen from the north. Source: Photo by Benjamin Lawson, all rights reserved.

Etzl Museum. Source: Photo by Benjamin Lawson, all rights reserved.

Hassan Bek Mosque seen from Charles Clore Park. Source: Photo by Benjamin Lawson, all rights reserved.

Neve Tzedek. Source: Photo by Benjamin Lawson, all rights reserved.

Neve Tzedek. Source: Photo by Benjamin Lawson, all rights reserved.

The White City. Source: Photo by Benjamin Lawson, all rights reserved.

Beit Ha'ir, Tel Aviv's first City Hall. Source: Photo by Benjamin Lawson, all rights reserved.

Mayor's office, Beit Ha'ir. Source: Photo by Benjamin Lawson, all rights reserved.

View of Bialik St. from the Mayor's Office, Beit Ha'ir. Source: Photo by Benjamin Lawson, all rights reserved.

View from rooftop balcony, Beit Ha'ir. Source: Photo by Benjamin Lawson, all rights reserved.

Vacant building with graffiti, central Tel Aviv. Source: Photo by Benjamin Lawson, all rights reserved.

Carmel Market. Source: Photo by Benjamin Lawson, all rights reserved.

Rothschild Boulevard. Source: Photo by Benjamin Lawson, all rights reserved.

Skyscrapers in Central Tel Aviv. Source: Photo by Benjamin Lawson, all rights reserved.

Skyscrapers along the Ayalon Expressway, seen from northern Tel Aviv. Source: Photo by Benjamin Lawson, all rights reserved.

Hayarkon Street. Source: Photo by Benjamin Lawson, all rights reserved.

City Hall, Rabin Square. Source: Photo by Benjamin Lawson, all rights reserved.

Tel Aviv Museum of Art. Source: Photo by Benjamin Lawson, all rights reserved.

Plaza by the Museum of Art. Source: Photo by Benjamin Lawson, all rights reserved.

Houses in North Tel Aviv. Source: Photo by Benjamin Lawson, all rights reserved.

Hotels along the beaches. Source: Photo by Benjamin Lawson, all rights reserved.

Tel Aviv Marina. Source: Photo by Benjamin Lawson, all rights reserved.

North Tel Aviv. Source: Photo by Benjamin Lawson, all rights reserved.

Hayarkon Park at sunset. Source: Photo by Benjamin Lawson, all rights reserved.

Bridge over the Yarkon River. Source: Photo by Benjamin Lawson, all rights reserved.

Boardwalk, near Tel Aviv Port. Source: Photo by Benjamin Lawson, all rights reserved.

Tel Aviv Port, Reading D Plant in background. Source: Photo by Benjamin Lawson, all rights reserved.

Hiriya (top left) seen from Ben-Gurion International Airport. Source: Photo by Benjamin Lawson, all rights reserved.

Back Cover

Photo of Benjamin A. Lawson by Aihua Zheng.

Index

CPSIA information can be obtained
at www.ICGtesting.com
Printed in the USA
LVOW02s1801290817
546735LV00005B/8/P

9 780977 244836